The Western Book of
CROSSING OVER

OTHER BOOKS BY SHELDON STOFF

Universal Kabbalah: Dawn of a New Consciousness
The Two-Way Street
The Human Encounter, Vols. I and II
The Pumpkin Quest

OTHER BOOKS BY JOSHUA J. STOFF

Building Moon-Ships
Long Island Airports
The Grumman Lunar Module
Aviation Firsts
Transatlantic Flight
Charles Lindbergh
Early Aviation
World War II Aircraft Production
Chariots for Apollo
Dirigible

The Western Book of
CROSSING OVER

Conversations with the Other Side

SHELDON STOFF

Foreword by Barbara Smith Stoff • Illustrations by Joshua Jordan Stoff

Frog Books
Berkeley, California

Published by Frog Books
Frog Books' publications are distributed by
North Atlantic Books
P.O. Box 12327
Berkeley, California 94712

Cover and book design by Suzanne Albertson
Printed in the United States of America

The Western Book of Crossing Over: Conversations with the Other Side is sponsored by the Society for the Study of Native Arts and Sciences, a nonprofit educational corporation whose goals are to develop an educational and cross-cultural perspective linking various scientific, social, and artistic fields; to nurture a holistic view of arts, sciences, humanities, and healing; and to publish and distribute literature on the relationship of mind, body, and nature.

North Atlantic Books' publications are available through most bookstores. For further information, call 800-733-3000 or visit our website at www.northatlanticbooks.com.

Library of Congress Cataloging-in-Publication Data
Stoff, Sheldon.
    The western book of crossing over : conversations with the other side / Sheldon Ptaschevitch Stoff ; illustrations by Joshua Jordan Stoff.
        p. cm.
    Includes bibliographical references and index.
Summary: "Packed with fascinating details about the afterlife, The Western Book of Crossing Over builds on the foundation laid by popular psychic authors Sylvia Browne and John Edward, and serves as a passionate reminder of the importance of keeping an awareness of the 'other side' in order to live fully and authentically on this side of the life-death divide"— Provided by publisher.
    ISBN 978-1-58394-266-6
    1. Future life. 2. Parapsychology. I. Title.
BF1311.F8S83 2009
133.901 3—dc22   2009005928

1   2   3   4   5   6   7   8   9   Versa   14   13   12   11   10   09

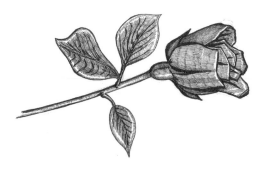

For Lorraine,
Who transmitted much of this book from the Other Side,
Who always walks the Beauty Path with a heart filled with love
and compassion. I love you.
—SHEL

For Shel,
From one soul to another, keep up the good work. Continue the path
and create the wonders. Love and kisses always and forever.
—LORRAINE

To the Wise One, my guide, I've always expressed
my gratitude to you. Now, I do so publicly.
Thank you with love,
—SHEL

ACKNOWLEDGMENTS

I n *Universal Kabbalah: Dawn of a New Consciousness,* we tried to make real the anchor in the physical world. In this book we tried to provide an understanding of the Other Side in order to continue to make real our anchor in this, our physical world. We must be anchored in both, the prelude and the forever act.

It can be said that in knowing that the here and there, this side and the Other, are both the Eternal One's creations, we can begin our unique task of hallowing this, our present life. Let us begin today with ourselves in relationship with others. This is the next chapter in the story of two entities in love who are called Lorraine and Sheldon. As this is written Lorraine is on the Other Side and Sheldon is still on Earth.

To Barbara Smith Stoff, who brings more than thirty years of concentration upon transpersonal and esoteric studies, I wish to offer a special thank you—for your careful and insightful reading of the manuscript, and for all your suggestions. To my editor Hisae Matsuda, many thanks for your caring and for your skill in moving the work through the difficulties of production. You're a pleasure to work with. To Kathy Glass, our copyeditor, your knowledge and thoughtfulness were in constant appreciation. Many, many thanks to all and especially to Richard Grossinger for keeping such a keen eye on the process.

SHELDON STOFF

"Man himself is the bridge between two worlds, and would cease to be human if he were anchored in only one of them."
—FRANZ WINKLER, MD, *Man: The Bridge Between Two Worlds*

"You know well enough, Man, what is good!
For what does the Lord require from you,
But to be just, to love mercy,
And to walk humbly with your God?"
—MICAH 6:8

CONTENTS

DRAWINGS OF THE OTHER SIDE

FOREWORD BY BARBARA SMITH STOFF

Although he had been fascinated with the concept of reincarnation—having begun, while still in his teens, with studies from the New York Psychic Society—Sheldon Stoff, who is now retired from university teaching in education and philosophy, had never thought to ask a question regarding the career and whereabouts of the soul between incarnations. In this book, he keeps company with such as C. S. Lewis (*A Grief Observed*), in that he finds himself in continuing contact with his deceased wife, Lorraine. During these surprising communications, Lorraine Marshak Stoff, who was married to Sheldon for more than fifty years, describes her experience of passing over, and then proceeds to go into details about the soul's ongoing experience and progress between lives.

There seemed to be some significance to the fact that Lorraine had chosen to cross over on my birthday in 2001, and that Shel and I had met on their wedding anniversary in 2004. Then we discovered that we had been pretty much on the same page with regard to teaching and public education in general all our professional lives, albeit he on the east coast, and I on the west coast. We each even held dog-eared copies of Richard Bach's *Jonathan Livingston Seagull,* which we used to broach similar topics in our lectures. He taught education and philosophy, while I taught literature and art. Dean Radin writes a lot about such "entanglement" over distances.

Here on Earth, somehow I think I must have signed on to help with the finishing up of an important task, especially in regard to Lorraine's meditative illuminated paintings depicting each of the letters of the Hebrew alphabet. Lorraine developed her medieval illumination techniques at the Metropolitan Museum in New York, and these paintings are her last work before she crossed over. She called them her "Mystical Interpretation of the Hebrew Alphabet." I feel a strong personal responsibility (a personal *tikkun,* if you will) to see that this lovely work finds a berth of honor—as a permanent exhibit in a museum and as a published book about them as well.

Throughout my life, it seems I have needed to ponder many puzzling pieces, and Gregg Braden's long, intense focus on bridging the voices of ancient wisdom and the modern world has been so very comforting to me. Even more coincidentally, it happens that for a great many years, I have been fascinated with the concept of the Hebrew alphabet as being a sacred alphabet based on sound and number. Gregg Braden treats this at length in *The God Code* (Carlsbad, CA: Hay House, 2005, illustrated edition), where he discusses a signature in our common DNA. I am hoping to soon come upon a similar exploration regarding Sanskrit—also a language based upon sacred sound and number. Aurobindo said, "At the core, in each cell, we are lit with God Light."

Asking a new kind of question can precipitate a profound change in our world view, and in our understanding of the entire cosmos. When we change our question, we begin to move forward in comprehension and toward greater spiritual evolution.

Today it seems that the whole world must to come to terms with a multi-national hydra-headed existential face-off. Thus it becomes, at this point in history, imperative that we work hard to educate ourselves, in order to gain some insight and understanding of our idea of ourselves as human beings in a very large universe, and how that idea is interpreted and played out on the increasingly communal world stage.

In our efforts to widen and deepen our concepts and understanding of life and meaning, it may be helpful if we place our inquiries within the larger questions posed by general systems theory. Directing an inquiring look at general systems theory and the nature of systems—how and why they organize themselves, and how they may change toward a more benevolent evolution—could help elucidate our own place in the larger universe.

Ervin Laszlo, often known as the father of systems science, says that as we now face a choice between "collapsing into chaos and evolving into a sustainable, ethical global community," the voices of the few, even the individual, can have a powerful effect for change. (*The Chaos Point: The World at the Crossroads,* Charlottesville, VA: Hampton Roads Publishing Company, Inc., 2006.) Scientists would say we are living in a "decision window"—a transitory period in the evolution of a system during which any input or influence, however small, can "blow up" to transform existing trends and bring new patterns and processes into existence. This is similar to the often-discussed "butterfly effect" discovered by U.S. meteorologist Edward Lorenz in the 1960s. In periods of relative stability, the consciousness of individuals does not play a decisive role in the behavior of society. But when a society reaches the limits of its stability and turns chaotic, it becomes super-sensitive—responsive to even small fluctuations such as changes in some people's values, beliefs, world views, and aspirations. Many signs point to the fact that we are entering a new period of ecological and social instability, a time rife with chaos but also a window of exceptional freedom to decide our destiny.

Reading history upon tragic history, and trying to comprehend truly and fairly, we think that now is the time to offer thoughts about strategies for a deeper healing at the heart of humankind. With Martin Buber and Vaclav Havel, we plead for benevolent evolution in our consciousness, in our understanding of who we are and where we are going. Are we evolving toward understanding and partnership?

Gregg Braden writes of "the existence of a field of energy—*The Divine Matrix*—that provides the container, as well as a bridge and mirror, for everything that happens between the world within us and the one outside of our bodies." Drawing upon theorists such as David Bohm and others within the discipline of quantum physics, Braden describes "deeper or higher planes of creation that hold the template for what happens in our world. It's from these subtler levels of reality that our physical world originates." He says:

The implication of both quantum theory and the ancient texts is that in the unseen realms we create the blueprint for the relationships, careers, successes, and failures of the visible world. From this perspective, the Divine Matrix works like a great cosmic screen that allows us to see the nonphysical energy of our emotions and beliefs (our anger, hate, and rage, as well as our love, compassion, and understanding) projected in the physical medium of life. (*The Divine Matrix: Bridging Time, Space, Miracles and Belief,* Carlsbad, CA: Hay House, Inc., 2007, p. xiv.)

If we look to ancient wisdom traditions and metaphysical writings, we find abundant theory on soul development. Having read deeply in the fields of esoterica for some forty years, I am excited to find validation in the fact that contemporary physicians, psychotherapists, and educators are now providing scientific support to ancient wisdom teachings regarding what we might call journeys of the soul. In particular, through the enduring and painstaking work of researchers such as David Chamberlain, Brian Weiss, and Michael Newton, there is now an expanding body of thought in the exploration of controversial issues involving our understanding of consciousness.

You can imagine my excitement and feeling of good fortune when I found myself in face-to-face dialogue with an individual who had the personal experience of an extended conversation with beings on the "other side." Sheldon's between-the-worlds dialogue with Lorraine can offer a response to essential questions and, as well, encourage us to keep on asking for more enlightenment regarding our situation and way of progress.

In his introduction, Gregg Braden goes on to say, "*The Divine Matrix* is written for those of you whose lives bridge the reality of our past with the hope of our future. It is you who are being asked to forgive and find compassion in a world reeling from the scars of hurt, judgment, and fear. The key to surviving our time in history is to create a new way of thinking while we're still living in the conditions that threaten our existence."

If Ervin Laszlo is right, and I think he is, in his *Chaos Point: The World at the Crossroads,* then such reporting of deep personal experience is extremely valuable at this time, in this critical "decision window." Carl Jung was fond of stressing that the experience of even one individual is statistically significant. It's staggering to contemplate that—but I often do and then look within myself for the courage to "belly up to the bar," as an old friend used to say.

To act in accord, to make a bridge to new ways of thinking, and in the belief that the reported experiences of individual journeys in consciousness can be of great significance now—at this point in time with the world in a general state of confrontation and conflict—we offer this story. It is within this frame of reflection that Sheldon's book, *The Western Book of Crossing Over: Conversations with the Other Side,* can be considered as making a vital statement for our progress toward a sustainable future here on Earth.

—BARBARA SMITH STOFF
LOOMIS, CALIFORNIA
FEBRUARY 2009

PREFACE

This is a book that I never expected to write. There is an old expression that says, "It just seemed to happen that way." We often accept that something just happens, perhaps by coincidence, yet I don't believe in coincidence. Let me explain how this book "just seemed to happen" and why it has been such a welcome surprise to me.

If you read *Universal Kabbalah: Dawn of a New Consciousness,* you know that my wife Lorraine made many contributions to that book *after* she had crossed over on April 18, 2001. Not one word of that book had been written before she crossed over. From the Other Side, she provided a perspective for the book that has helped many people, giving remarkable insights into a deeper and broader comprehension of life processes, and thus enabling them to live a more loving, productive life here on Earth.

Several peaceful months after *Universal Kabbalah* was completed, I was awakened early one weekend morning. Lorraine was talking to me about the next book that we would have to write, *The Western Book of Crossing Over: Conversations with the Other Side.* Peace was to give way to dedicated writing. This new book was to become my central task, as I gave up other work in order to be able to concentrate on the writing during most of my waking hours. I purchased a small digital tape recorder to capture the thoughts that might come while driving. Lorraine would often stand behind me when I worked at the computer, so that some of the descriptions became quite lengthy and were always awesome to me, the receiver.

In order to write this second book, Lorraine had pointed out that I would not simply receive dictation as I originally thought—that for this work, and any that might follow, I would need to continue growing in spiritual depth and sensitivity. I must develop the ability to introduce concepts about the Other Side by receiving help from the Other Side through silence and meditation, and I must also be able to draw illustrations with the help that the Other Side would provide. Then Joshua, my son, would use my rough drawings and descriptions as the basis for finished drawings, to be included in this book. I realized that the decision requiring my continued growth was very sound. I welcomed it.

Although this was an unplanned event in my life, this working with the Other Side was not completely astonishing to me. As a young student I read much material dealing with reincarnation from the New York Psychic Society. There were many incidents of personal remembering and communication spelled out in detail, so the possibility of reincarnation and communication with the Other Side seemed a very natural occurrence to me. Even so, during all my years prior to writing this book, I never gave much thought to what the Other Side was all about in a practical sense, so the contents of this book came as a great surprise to me.

An especially vivid memory comes to mind here. After I graduated from Long Island Ag and Tech, Lorraine and I purchased a poultry farm, and I often received messages from my late Uncle Sol, who had been a poultry farmer, giving me advice on the care of chickens. I still remember that surprising "voice" in my head one freezing cold night. I was in the coop with the baby chicks. It was three in the morning. "Learn to think like a chicken," my uncle suggested.

As a result of this advice, we broke records for egg production and low chicken mortality. We were even written up in a national poultry magazine. On reflection now, I think the self-discipline I had to master in order to care for those baby chicks enabled me to endure the later rigors of getting my doctorate at Cornell.

Throughout my life, from time to time, I received advice and even direct help when it was needed. My life was saved on at least two occasions, and I was often helped with suggestions when I earnestly sought guidance from the Other Side. This was always appreciated and was humbly accepted. I deemed this kind of communication a proper way to do things. Certainly, I thought, the Other Side can see matters more clearly, and it seems reasonable to admit this when I need help.

My ego is not so large that I should believe that I know it all.

I began to meditate and pray more concertedly for a truth not bound by nation, region, specific religion, or even gender. I believe, and there is much evidence to support this view, that if we are attached to a specific mind-set, this mind-set will be reflected in what we see and hear; thus it is important to go beyond our prior attachments and focus only upon the profound realization that *each of us is simply a child of the universe, and that it is necessary to proceed in meditation unadorned by past attachments.* In other words, have an open mind.

To be more specific, I believe that if we pray in the Jewish tradition, what we receive *will be within that tradition.* If we pray in the Catholic tradition, what we receive *will be within that tradition.* If we pray in the Vedic tradition, what we receive *will be within that tradition.* The list continues. If we want an unadorned truth, we must fully commit to truth and pray simply as a child of the universe. I believe that by seeking to encounter the spiritual as a child of the universe, with no particular religious attachments, even those of my own beloved Kabbalah, we can come closer to human and divine truth.

This statement does not mean that we forget the organized religions that cradled us in early years. Those early years need support, and there are tasks for religion to do. One of those tasks is to take us up to the gates of a deeper, more inclusive perception—love and compassion for all. From there we need to have the courage to go forth naked, without trappings. That is an awesome decision, not to be made lightly. Each of us must have the courage to go forth, to learn, to help, to receive, and to make our own decisions with love and humility.

I have meditated for some fifty years, and I am deeply grateful to Kabbalah for helping me to expand my consciousness and for fostering my spiritual growth. After all these years, I've gotten pretty good at silencing my mind and just quietly and calmly listening. Listening in harmony was my goal. At some point, years ago, I realized that to fully encounter the Other Side, I had to go forward unencumbered. I had to be free of any attitudinal attachments that might influence what I might receive in meditations. This insight was a wonderful realization. To be fully open to receive in meditation I had to honestly present myself as a child of the universe, a child of God filled with love, and learn to appreciate truth no matter where it led. This was a turning point in my life. *I cherished my new freedom of action. I believe that now I can move toward a fuller understanding of the implications of my freedom on the Earth as a loving, spiritual Being having a human incarnation.*

As I began to write this second book, I was reminded of a graduate class I taught at Adelphi University some years ago. It was the first night and I read aloud the list of philosophers that we would be studying that semester. I included John Dewey and his concept of freedom, which has become the American understanding of freedom for many in the United States. A student in the back of the room raised her hand and said that she wouldn't read Dewey. I replied that it did not matter to me if she praised or condemned Dewey, as long as her critique was sound. Her answer was one that I had never heard before in all my years of teaching. She said that because her pastor had said that "Dewey was devilish" she would not read him.

I explained that narrowness at the beginning of a quest denies the purpose of the quest itself, and that one of the purposes of a university education is to expose students to varying points of view, and that I believe that understanding several points of view is essential to growth, and even to democracy. I also explained that I would never suggest that she accept any particular position, that I would offer seven or eight views on the subject, and that her responsibility would be to learn to think things through for herself. She again said that she would not read Dewey. I suggested that if she were unwilling to read various points of view in order to gain greater insight and perspective regarding a subject, she ought to drop the class and save herself some money. This she did.

As I go back to my dialogue with Lorraine, I relate this now in order to emphasize that there is nothing that follows here that a reader must accept, but there is indeed a great deal to think about as a prelude to choices and actions along a path.

Having read *The Tibetan Book of the Dead* and *The Egyptian Book of the Dead,* I wondered to Lorraine if we, in our writing *The Western Book of Crossing Over,* would be able to bring forth new information that would help people live more authentic and productive lives on Earth. Lorraine gave me a quick "yes" and drew away. The information would not follow any prescribed doctrine. There would be no attachment to any previous religious conditioning. The transmissions would be only as lengthy as necessary to have an understanding of the Other Side. They would be simple, precise, and very helpful to those who would "just happen" to find the book in their hands.

We will read descriptions of activities on the Other Side that will enable us to more fully understand who we are and why we are here on Earth, thus helping us to fulfill our individual mission and learn unconditional love. Apparently what concerns the Other Side is the love and compassion in our hearts and actions, not the particular religion we may happen to affiliate with during any particular incarnation. I know that what we usually understand has a time-specific quality to it. Thus it is understood, and lived, within a current culture. Know then, that these books, *Universal Kabbalah* and *The Western Book of Crossing Over,* were written to help people make each incarnation one of growth and enjoyment, one of caring, one of helping and healing, one of thinking and acting in love—a journey of inner freedom, of being fully alert and responsible at all times.

Lorraine has said that this second book is an important part of our writing books together, but not the conclusion of my writing or of my physical life. This writing has been a grand journey, and I am delighted to share it with you. It was planned that way. These insights are not written for angels but are insights into how we humans may live our lives here on Earth. Living a humble and wholesome life is a practical way to follow a path toward spiritual harmony and maturity. At the core of this life is our complete responsibility for our actions. Our "Life Review," shortly after crossing over, will make that abundantly clear to each and every one of us. There is no escape from our responsibility for our actions, as well as our omissions. Our ability to act with care, love, and compassion is essential to our spiritual growth.

Such spiritual awareness should help us to live a more appropriate existence and to fill life with richness, not boredom or apathy. Spiritual awareness will also affect our life when we return to the Other Side. Both sides form a whole and are intertwined just as we can be entangled with significant others here on this side of the veil. Remember, we are, at all times, spiritual beings having a human experience for growth. Our actions can be appropriate to that understanding, at least as appropriate as we can make them at any particular time in our development. Our journey is always a spiritual one—of free will, healing, devotion, compassion and discovery, active (not passive) loving, and participation, not simply contemplation. Our journey flows out from our inner consciousness and our relationships with others. It is a reaching for Cosmic Consciousness, a quest to fully comprehend that all of us, and all that there is, is in the eternal One!

Let me share a delightful story that will tell you something about consciousness and things shared between Earth and the Other Side. Among Lorraine's accomplishments, she was a skilled porcelain artist. One evening she was at her art desk beginning to paint a porcelain pin. I remarked that it was time to go to bed, and she asked me to go alone and said that she would follow in "ten minutes." Six hours later I awoke to find her still at her bench. The pin was just completed so it was finally her bedtime.

About a year later we were at a party in her sister's garden. Lorraine and I were on one side of a large group when she happened to spot one of her sister's friends wearing a stunning porcelain pin. She remarked to me that it had to be an expensive antique pin. She had to see it close up. We approached the woman and Lorraine complimented her on the magnificent pin. The friend looked astonished. "You painted it" was her reply. Lorraine still did not remember painting that pin, but her initials in the lower right corner told her that indeed this came from her own tiny brush.

I believe that we sometimes fail to realize how often we are actually cooperating with unseen spiritual beings when we are involved in creating something. The hours go by swiftly, unnoticed by memory, as we are transported to another level of consciousness altogether.

In concluding this preface, I want to emphasize a point that Lorraine dwelled upon. The main purpose of this book is to demonstrate that we, *every single one of us,* are all spiritual beings within a physical body. At our core we are Spirit. Since we are viewing here a greater picture than just life on Earth, we will have a glimpse of the Other Side. It is given to provide all of us with the courage to act here *from our souls* with helpfulness, love, compassion, and responsibility. Learning such new habits will set free our love, and we will know that every part of life is to be cherished.

Keep in mind that the experience on the Other Side is REALITY. It has a permanence that we lack here. Yes! It is also a major site for reflection, listening, learning, and loving. As in Plato's allegory of the cave, it is the sunshine beyond the shadow existence on Earth. What you experience in your reading of this book can be the motivation that fully awakens you to the glory of this life with all its fascinating and wonderful dimensions.

At the heart of the matter is our consciousness. When we depart from Earth, we go only with our consciousness and no material possessions—think of what that means. If we have experienced Cosmic Consciousness, even a little during our Earthly journey, our trip back home will be much smoother and our stay there much more awesome. An actively involved consciousness of love and compassion not only allows us to be one with the Light, it also brings an enhanced love to our beautiful planet and to *all* its inhabitants.

If not you, who?
If not now, when?
—*Hillel*
(This legendary sage reportedly lived just before
the time of Jesus and came from the House of Hillel.)

Much of our early history has been distorted, especially our knowledge
of religion and gender. Our civilization needs a "major correction."
We know that there have been many additions, omissions, and changes
in scriptural accounts of our heritage. It is always our task to seek that
which is eternal and to discard that which has been severely redacted or
was meant for a specific time and place.

All religions can contribute to a more complete knowledge of what
life is about. No one religion has all the answers. They have all suffered
major distortions that obscure their valuable beginnings. Our varied
experiences in the different religions and incarnations are all for our
growth. Religions have a supreme purpose of taking us to embrace the
spiritual and each other in every day and every way. A religion is like a
train taking us to a destination. The destination is the goal. A specific
train is only one vehicle, of several, headed toward that destination.

Reading this book may be your chosen train or vehicle. It may help
you to get to your destination. To love the eternal One and all of God's
creations is a formidable goal. Please don't become satisfied with just
reading details about the Other Side. Embrace the knowledge that you
are a spiritual being living through a physical incarnation and go forth,
welcoming freedom, spiritual growth, healing, and responsibility. Go
beyond where you are. Open your eyes and begin to flower in your daily
existence. You are that rose, a thing of beauty, and a joy to behold. In
this incarnation, you may have selected a "Sabbath" as your holy day,
but remember that all days are holy. All of life is holy. Every hour and
every minute falls into that category. An honest, open commitment to
a chosen spiritual path will, in itself, bring you a newfound joy. You

will begin to understand why you are here. The world will become a fresh vista. Your openness will be a leap forward in loving insight.

It is fair to say in commenting on our current time that modern life, with its daily entertainments, distracts us from a clear focus. Silence is a vital part of our being. We all know the saying "Silence is golden." It enables our channels to be open to *reception* from the Other Side. I strongly recommend the continuation of our history of meditation as one way of encountering the Akashic Field.*

Think of an egg as representing all of religion and spiritual life. Religion is just the shell. The entire egg is our spiritual life. We must not take the shell as the whole egg and remain unaware of the substance inside the egg. The lasting nourishment is to be found inside the shell. That which is *inside* is the goal to which our religions should take us, and meditation is one of the chief vehicles. We might say, then, that a balanced spiritual life—the whole egg—may include a wide variety of experiences, activities, and practices. We are here to enjoy and to learn.

There are endless opportunities to learn to love and respect each other. Time here on Earth is very precious. Nothing should be taken for granted. We can choose to become aware and grow in every moment. All time and space is holy, even this very moment when you are reading this. Every person deserves a chance, an opportunity for spiritual growth. This includes you and me. Education on the Other Side is described later in the book and makes the journey more understandable.

When you see the shift in type style, you will know that I am directly quoting Lorraine, although I am sure that what I say after prayers and meditation is also under the influence and acceptance of the Other Side. The beings on the Other Side provide us with suggestions for living a truly noble life and a way to climb the ladder of an expanded consciousness.

*The Akashic Field, first described in Sanskrit about five thousand years ago, is the beginning of all and the end of all. It also houses the memory of all that has ever happened.

There is, of course, more to know regarding life on the Other Side, but we will all experience that in due time. In the meantime, as we mature spiritually, what we conceive to be true will have to change, to deepen and widen. Our actions must also mature. It all must begin wherever we are "at" mentally, and then we grow as we walk through life, coming more and more to understand the richness of existence in all its forms and dimensions.

As above, so below.

As below, so above.

—SHELDON STOFF
TUCSON, ARIZONA
JANUARY 2008

CHAPTER 1

Reincarnation

"The soul that has fulfilled its task, that has done what it has to do in terms of creating or repairing its own part of the world and realizing its own essence, can wait after death for the perfection of the world as a whole. But not all the souls are so privileged: many stray for one reason or another; sometimes a person does not do all the proper things, and sometimes he misuses forces and spoils his portion and the portion of others. In such cases, the soul does not complete its task and may even itself be damaged by contact with the world. It has not managed to complete that portion of reality which only this particular soul can complete; and therefore after the death of the body, the soul returns and is reincarnated in the body of another person and again must try and complete what it failed to correct or what it injured in the past. The sins of man are not eliminated so long as this soul does not complete that which it has to complete."

—RABBI ADIN STEINSALTZ,
THE THIRTEEN-PETALLED ROSE[1]

You may think it odd that I begin this book by repeating or drawing upon much of the content of two chapters from our previous book, *Universal Kabbalah: Dawn of a New Consciousness*. Understanding the concept of reincarnation is essential to a full spiritual understanding. Spiritual growth requires continuous learning experiences provided by reincarnation. We're simply trying to provide here in these pages a context in which to function. You may already realize the distilled truth of many incarnations here on Earth, which were designed for your growth and healing. You always have good, positive reasons for coming to Earth. Now you will have a better understanding of the essential nature of the Other Side and why many physical incarnations have been a must for each of us.

We always make our own decisions regarding frame and circumstance of our many incarnations, which are necessary for our maturity. We have all experienced lives with other religions, other nationalities, other sexes, and other social classes. These have all been part of our necessary growth process. We should all understand that bigotry is stupidity since we probably were once that which we may now frown upon. If you were not before, you can be pretty sure that you will be in the future what you hate now. What an effective way to learn tolerance. An extended family understanding is in order for all of us.

As a boy I instinctively understood the reality of reincarnation, even though this vital concept had never been discussed in Hebrew School. In fact today many rabbis, reverends, and priests still don't know of the long history of the concept of reincarnation within Judaism, Christianity, and Islam. In all major esoteric pathways reincarnation is fully accepted and understood as far as humanly possible. When I do a spiritual retreat before non-Jewish clergy or have lunch with a priest or minister, I have never been challenged on the concept. In a quiet time, perhaps over tea and cookies, a clergyman has often said to me, "I believe as you do but it's not church doctrine, so I can't speak of it with my congregation."

Many new clergy from all denominations, and some who have been around for a long time, understand that the evidence supporting reincarnation is overwhelming. *It is the only spiritual concept that I'm aware of that is publicly verifiable.* Some of us understand it from the inside. We accept it because we accept memories of one or more past lives.

Some time ago I went for a spiritual reading by Ted Silverhand, a well-known Native American Seer from North Carolina, who was then in Ithaca, New York. He has a distinguished record of accurate readings. One of his first comments to me was: "You were an Indian medicine man in your last life and your current wife [Lorraine] was also your wife then. You had such a great marriage that you decided to come back together again. Just before that incarnation you were a rabbi and Lorraine was also with you."

I then understood why the attraction was so strong between Lorraine and me in the fifth grade. We *had* come back together again! It's great that it worked out that way. When I look around my living room now, and I'm barely counting the other rooms, it's easy to confirm what Ted said about my Native American heritage. I lived in the middle of it and didn't realize it.

About twenty years ago I meditated on Lorraine's past incarnation. I told her that she had been an Indian woman living on the central plains of North America. I never thought to ask if I was in the picture. All the items listed below were acquired *prior* to my telling Lorraine of her previous incarnation.

- We have five hand-woven Native American rugs; one hanging on our living room wall measures 4 x 6 feet.
- We have three hand-made Indian Kachinas on a shelf, two quite large and beautifully decorated. They are of museum quality.
- There is one awesome Indian carving on the living room wall.
- There are three Indian beaded pendants hanging on our dining room wall.
- There is one Indian feather pendant hanging on our living room wall.
- There's a long Indian peace pipe on a bookcase shelf.
- I own nine silver Indian bolos (to replace neckties).
- I own an Indian carved-bone eagle head bolo of museum quality.
- There's an eagle feather, given to me by Victor Sarracino of Laguna Pueblo. He said at the time he gave it to me, "You're more Indian than many of my people."
- I often wear Eagle T-Shirts in honor of my totem, an Eagle.
- There are twenty-nine Indian tapes as part of our music collection.
- We have a "black pot" and a wedding vase purchased on a reservation.
- I own three Indian silver belt buckles.

- We own approximately a hundred books by or about Indians.
- Lorraine and I were scheduled to do a workshop at Cornell University with Ron LaFrance, then a chief of the Roosevelt Town reservation.
- I own a medicine bag that I have kept filled with the appropriate herbs, etc., for more than forty years.
- Lorraine has two miniature dioramas of Navajo women weaving.
- Lorraine took a course in Navajo weaving and we built a six-foot-tall Navajo loom.
- I made a teacher-training film at Laguna Pueblo, New Mexico.
- I have a beautiful Indian God's Eye hanging in my study.
- I have an Indian Healing Mask, of museum quality, hanging in my study.
- While Lorraine was teaching art at the university, she had several classes make their own God's Eye.
- I own a silver Indian-made ring.
- On vacations we often visited Indian Reservations.
- We've made many visits to Indian museums and trading posts.
- We have a framed Indian "item" behind our bed indicating the plants traditionally obtained for color for Indian rugs.
- Lorraine owns a lovely Indian Squash Blossom and a great deal of Indian-made jewelry.
- I closed my university classes with an Indian prayer to the Four Winds. I opened them with Indian flute playing in order to separate our class from outside distractions.
- Lorraine loves the aroma of sage and often burns sage smudge sticks. I find that burning sage incense when meditating is a big help.

Remember, we are two kids from Brooklyn. We weren't collecting. These were simply items that we needed to have. We never even thought about what these things might have said to us if we only looked around and listened. I still marvel that I created my own medicine bag.

In order to flesh out the concept of reincarnation, I will attempt to show a progression in consciousness. I will first look at Near-Death Experiences (NDE) as described by Carol Zalesti[2] and others to note that consciousness *does not cease* upon clinical death. This is our first step on the road to understanding reincarnation, the road of Eternal Life and an expanded consciousness.

Pollster George Gallup, Jr., found that eight million adults in the United States have had an NDE.[3] That equals one person in twenty. He was further able to analyze the content of each NDE by polling for their specific elements. Here is what he found:

ELEMENT	PERCENT
Out of body	26
Accurate visual perception	23
Audible sounds or voices	17
Feelings of peace, painlessness	32
Light phenomena	14
Life review	32
Being in another world	32
Encountering other beings	23
Tunnel experience	9
Recognition	6

I often had a discussion of the near-death experience with my university classes when it was appropriate. It was a rare class where someone present, or an immediate family member, had not had a classic NDE. When students saw a peer describing such an experience with tears running down his/her cheeks, a decided change in awareness became very evident.

Generally, books whose subject is the NDE provide many quotations by individuals who have had such an experience. At times, these experiences are authenticated by police or firemen when appropriate. Some of these experiences are detailed and quite lengthy. Some people describe accidents, floating in air, meeting with another being, a tunnel experience and/or meeting a light entity asking them to return to their body.

What follows is a description of one experience in order to give you an insight into the phenomenon.

> One woman left her body, went into the waiting room, and saw that her daughter was wearing mismatched plaids. What had happened was that the maid had brought the child to the hospital and in her haste had grabbed the first two things off the laundry pile. Later, when she told her family about her experience and the fact that she had seen the girl in these mismatched clothes, they knew that she must have been in that waiting room.[4]

In reading books about Near-Death Experiences we see that a few things stand out:

- The importance of sharing information about the NDE when the individual returns to local consciousness.
- Knowing the supreme value of being loved by spiritual reality when in one's physical state.
- Knowing the importance of sharing and caring here on Earth.
- Knowing that everyone and everything in the universe is connected.

Afterlife researcher Dr. Raymond Moody's final line in his book *Life After Life* sums up what is likely an insight for all of us to take to our hearts: "[We] cannot fully understand this life until we catch a glimpse of what lies beyond it."[5]

The evidence that consciousness does not need a physical body has been our starting point. It is an important step in our discussion of reincarnation. It is relatively easy to understand the reality of reincarnation by proceeding carefully. Many of us have experienced steps along its progression, so we can validate it from the inside. We also have many,

many insights provided by the detailed investigations undertaken by others. Some of these will be related here. From this side of creation it is impossible to fully grasp all the nuances.

Rabbi Lawrence Kushner, with perceptive thought, adds to the complexity of the concept when he states:

> Sooner or later, in one lifetime or another,
> Each soul must accomplish its intended task. . . .[6]
> Never forget that you too yourself may be a messenger.
> Perhaps, even one whose errand extends over several lifetimes.[7]

Those famous in history who have discussed reincarnation from the inside read like a "who's who" of philosophical and religious thinking. I list just a few of the many in order to demonstrate that it is not simply a narrow spectrum of humanity who lived reincarnation's progression:

Plato
Pythagoras
Rabbi Eliyahu of Vilna (the Vilna Gaen)
Professor Quincy Howe, Jr. (Reincarnation for the Christian)
Dr. Rudolf Frieling (Christianity and Reincarnation)
Rabbi Isaac Luria
Rabbi Shimon Bar Yochai
Rabbi Moshe de Leon
Rabbi Hayim Vital
General George Patton
Josephus, the famous Jewish historian (37–93 CE)

> *"Do ye not remember at all pure spirits who are in conformity with the divine . . . and in the course of time they are again sent down to inhabit sinless bodies."*
> —JOSEPHUS

With Joseph Head and S.L. Cranston's monumental work, *Reincarnation: The Phoenix Fire Mystery*, we have two scientists whose work has been published in scholarly and scientific journals. Quotations are included from the Hebrew Scriptures, the New Testament, and various other religious sources. A discussion of how this belief about reincarnation became divorced from Christian teachings is also presented there. In order to fit an example into this chapter I've selected a short experience rather than a more detailed view that you might pursue on your own. The following case of supposed remembrance was among the first reported by afterlife researcher Dr. Ian Stevenson, and it appeared with others in his published essay "The Evidence for Survival from Claimed Memories of Former Incarnations":[8]

The Case of Eduardo Esplugus-Cubrera: A four-year-old boy who lived in Havana told his parents about a home and different parents he claimed to have had in a previous life. His statements taken together gave the following items of information.

When I lived at 69 Rue Campanario, my father's name was Pierro Seco, and my mother's Amparo. I recollect that I had two little brothers with whom I used to play, and whose names were Mercedes and Jean. The last time that I went out of the house was Sunday, 28th February, 1903, and my mother then cried a great deal while I was leaving the house. This other mother of mine had a very clear complexion and black hair. She used to make hats. I was then thirteen and I bought drugs at the American chemist's because they were cheaper than the other shops. I left my little bicycle in the room below when I came back from my walk. I was not called Eduardo as I am now, but Pancho.

The parents were sure the boy had never been to the house he named. To test the matter they made a long detour to reach the street where the house was, this house being quite unfamiliar to them and, so they firmly believed, should have been to the boy also. On arrival at the street, the boy immediately recognized the house as the one about which he had been talking. They encouraged the boy to enter the house, but he found it occupied by strangers whom he did not recognize. The parents then made further inquires about the previous occupants of the house and uncovered the following facts.

Number 69 Rue Campanario was occupied until a short time after the month of February 1903 by Antonio Seco who had by then (1907) left Havana. Señor Seco had a wife called Amparo and three sons called Mercedes, Jean, and Pancho. Pancho had died in the month of February 1903.[9]

As a teenager I did have a teenager's grasp of reincarnation. I thought then and I believe now that religion and spirituality make no sense without understanding the place of reincarnation to complete the picture. There's simply too much to know and so much to mature that it can't be accomplished in only one attempt. The books by the New York Psychic Society, read in my teens, provided another avenue for understanding reincarnation with their detailed accounts of multiple lives.

I've also pointed out in my presentations on the subject that reincarnation is the one concept that makes spirituality come alive. Again, the evidence is overwhelming, both on the inside and in the public arena. If you still have doubts, start looking at the evidence. The Head and Cranston book is a good place to begin.

I list here a few random thoughts on the subject:

- We select our parents, usually to help us with a task or healing in a particular incarnation.
- We can learn from both positive and negative experiences.
- Thankfully, we're given more than one chance to learn and mature spiritually.

- We can't avoid growth. If we don't handle a problem properly, we come back to a similar situation and try to solve it again. This can be repeated until we get it right. An extended period of time may elapse between incarnations in order for us to have time to dwell upon a subject or a past life.

I'd like to close this chapter, not with hard evidence, but with a few brief thoughts on the subject by some very trustworthy people:

". . . reincarnation has vast potential. It is not a punishment for sin as much as an opportunity to raise any of the sparks that have not been redeemed . . ."
—RABBI DAVID COOPER[10]

"Kabbalah teaches that we will return to this world in many incarnations until we achieve complete transformation."
—RABBI MICHAEL BERG[11]

"It will be necessary to direct our attention first to the fact of Christ's existence, which is basic for all Christianity. Then it will be seen that the idea of reincarnation, though not applicable to Christ Himself, is all the more so to mankind's becoming Christian."
—DR. RUDOLF FRIELING[12]

"The doctrine of reincarnation provides the script for a drama of cosmic proportions: it accounts for the source of the individual soul, the demands and conditions for its self-improvement, and the final goal of the journey."
—DR. QUINCY HOWE, JR.[13]

"I chose this time period to be born because it is a great period of change where people need stability within themselves. I am supposed to help them somehow. I did choose to become a male, because it is good for my work, and I enjoy that sex role. My mother was my wife in a past life, my father was my son. I got some faint flashes of mates or lovers, but nothing clear." (Statement from a participant in a workshop involving past-life regression.)
—*LIFE BEFORE LIFE* BY DR. HELEN WAMBACH[14]

"Master of the Universe! I hereby forgive anyone who has angered or vexed me, or sinned against me, either physically or financially, against my honor or anything else that is mine, whether accidentally or intentionally, inadvertently or deliberately, by speech or by deed, in this incarnation or in any other. . . ."
—RABBI NISSEN MANGEL, TRANSLATING FROM *SIDDUR TEHILLAT HASHEM,* A HEBREW PRAYER BOOK[15]

Personally, as I looked back on three incarnations that I'm aware of, I tried to find a thread that has persisted in all of them. It was not difficult to locate. *"Love God and all of God's creations."*

CHAPTER 2

Your Mission on Earth

"Reincarnation from one body to another is a long and arduous quest for tikkun which the soul undergoes tens, even hundreds of times before it finally achieves its ultimate perfection and receives its rewards."
—RABBI DOVBER PINSON[1]

"It is as if a king had sent you to a country to carry out one special, specific task. You go to the country and perform a hundred other tasks, but if you have not performed the task you were sent for, it is as if you have performed nothing at all. So man has come into the world for a particular task, and that is his purpose. If he doesn't perform it, he will have done nothing."
—RUMI

Almost all of this chapter comes from our previous book, *Universal Kabbalah: Dawn of a New Consciousness*. Each of us has decided to come to Earth, to be reborn for good and positive reasons, perhaps a healing, perhaps to write a book, perhaps to learn to overcome adversity. Knowing this, we now have some background with which to review our present situation and awaken to the charge we placed upon ourselves when we could see more clearly. There is never a dull day when we realize that we have much to do in the short time that we are here. We have a responsibility unique to us alone. There is a task that we have chosen and for which we are grateful. We are given another chance to help fulfill our destiny. Proceed with joy in your heart, for this mission involves the whole of your Earthly existence. You are the reason why you are here!

As strange as it seems, you and I have selected precisely where we are today (if we have not strayed), and today we have everything available to us to complete our individual mission. In the tradition of Kabbalah, there is a term, "tikkun." So, what is a tikkun?

- *Tikkun* = Your mission or purpose on Earth. Your ability to heal yourself and others from past deeds incurred in previous

incarnations. Your need to learn your lessons for spiritual
growth.

• *Tikkun Olam* = Healing the world by your deeds.

Our mission or purpose exists on many levels:

The prime purpose for all of us in every incarnation is to learn to
love God and to learn to share God's love.

To love the spark of God in everyone and everything.

To turn, to heal myself and others, perhaps having suffered in
previous incarnations.

To grow spiritually by learning needed lessons and living nobly
and responsibly.

To live a joyous incarnation as a *Child of the Universe.*

To learn to function in love and harmony in a place devoid of love
and harmony.

In understanding the concept of mission, we can begin to more fully
experience the reason for the creation of the universe. It was and is to
allow each of us to learn to love. There are no exceptions to this rule.
God's spark within, the soul, is always pure in its upper levels. Lower
levels can be harmed by listening to the self-centered ego. Physical creation allows us to develop nobility in our lives—a concept of glorious
beauty and responsibility. At the heart of every incarnation is bathing
in love and harmony. Only when we awaken to reality, which is God's
love in each of us, can we begin to function well in this incarnation.
Then we have a reason to cast off self-centeredness and embrace all of
God's creations. We can begin to fulfill our individual mission.

This concept is completely intertwined with that of reincarnation,
as the previous chapter demonstrated. The following statement by Dr.
Joel Whitton adds support to the seriousness of the concept of mission:

Total self-responsibility may be perceived as freedom on the edge of
a razor, but the terror is mitigated by the knowledge that we are all

partaking in an awesome evolutionary process that invests each thought, word, and deed with meaning and purpose.[2]

Later in this chapter I offer suggestions for awakening to your mission if you are unaware of it.

"For each and every human being has a specific task to perform in the World, a task that no one else can accomplish, though there may well be better and more gifted people around to do it. Only he can do it in a certain way, in the singular composite of manner, personality, and circumstance that belongs to him."[3]

"The significance of the past can be changed only at the higher level of repentance called Tikkun."[4]
—RABBI ADIN STEINSALTZ

There is yet another significance to our understanding of this concept of mission. Its implications are eye-opening in their importance. What we accomplish on Earth counts. It is of such fundamental meaning to our maturity that it follows us to the Other Side. It *affects* who we will be with and our growth there, as it has affected our maturity here. Our existence on the Other Side is directly related to our existence, our knowledge, thoughts and actions right here on Earth. Similarly, our time there helps prepare us for our time here. *As above, so below. As below, so above.*

Lorraine passed over to the Other Side on April 18, 2001. We have been in contact more than forty times since then. On July 23, 2001, she told me that she was doing her art work on the topic of "God's love" and trying "to figure out what the universe is all about." Before crossing over, she had finished a magnificent painting series on "The Mystical Interpretation of the Hebrew Letters" just prior to having a stroke. In the hospital she told me that when she got home she would start another series on "God's love." Her desires had not changed—only where she would call home.

In a meditation on August 11, 2001, I succeeded in contacting Lorraine. I asked about her research on the universe. She replied, "So far, it's all about love."

Lorraine is a special, highly evolved spiritual individual. It's clear that she has been able to carry her interests over to the Other Side and also to bring those interests into her incarnations on Earth.

> *"If a man has not acquired merit in this world he will not acquire it any more in the other world."*
> —THE *ZOHAR*, MIQEZ, 196B

Our mission here prepares us for what we can accomplish here and there. We come only for healing and spiritual growth. It is always positive in nature, and we never plan on doing harm to another. If we do it is because we have deviated from our mission. All authentic communications from the spiritual domain are compassionate and loving. Any negativity that enters even a scripture tells us more about the author than about the spiritual. If our mission brings us pain, it may be because we are going through a time of enhanced spiritual growth. There are many possibilities for an action. A life of joy in the eternal One and in all of God's creations will accomplish the same purpose. Our mission here can extend over several incarnations in order for us to receive the necessary preparation.

> *"Meeting with God does not come to man in order that he may concern himself with God, but in order that he may confirm that there is meaning in the world. All revelation is summons and sending. . . ."*

> *"God remains present to you when you have been sent forth; he who goes on a mission has always God before him: the truer the fulfillment, the stronger and more constant His nearness."*
> —MARTIN BUBER[5]

When you fully turn to God, the world changes.

Let me share with you a true story that occurred in days long ago when I was teaching Agricultural Science at the high school level. I change only the names in order to protect the privacy of individuals.

One of my students, a tall boy named Phil, was due to be sent to prison because he had stolen a good many items that totaled about $25,000. Phil had been tried and found guilty and was sentenced to jail time. He refused to admit to the theft.

The day prior to his being sent to jail I asked Phil to see me after school. He came to my homeroom, an addition to the school that had recently been constructed for our new classroom and shop.

We sat down together on a bench outside. I was silent, looking at Phil, thinking of what I might say that hadn't been said before. Finally, I said, "Phil, why are you here?"

Phil looked at me strangely and answered, "Mr. Stoff, you asked me to come."

Well, that didn't work. Still at a loss for words I asked the same question again, just a little bit louder.

After a while, Phil replied again, looking a little worried: "Mr. Stoff, you asked me to come."

I had struck out twice. Still unsure of what to say, I thought and then blurted out: "Phil, why were you born?"

Phil looked shocked, excused himself, and ran into the hall promising to come right back. After ten minutes I went into the hall looking for a very frightened boy. I found Phil standing in a corner, crying. We hugged and he spoke tearfully, "I wasn't born to be a thief."

Later that day Phil returned all of the items that he had stolen, and his jail time was voided. With his new insight on life, he blossomed. Once he realized that he wasn't born to be a thief, he was able to explore positive alternatives, and many doors now opened before him. One seemed a dream. The dream did come true. He became a leader in the Future Farmers of America organization, which he loved, and he won the county "public speaking" competition. His leadership abilities began to mature. He had awakened from his sleep and now saw a destination to his life. He had found his mission on Earth.

> *"We did not appear in this world by chance. According to Kabbalistic teaching, we chose our present incarnation as a vehicle for completing our tikkun—a word that can be variously translated as the correction, or repair—or in order for our transformation to be attained.*
>
> *"What an astonishing idea this is! It means that you alone are the cause of who you are."*
> —RABBI MICHAEL BERG[6]

You and I are responsible for what we do. We truly are *co-creators* with God, especially on the Other Side. . . . God gives us free will. We are free to choose. We are responsible for our choices. We always select a positive mission as reason for incarnating, though we too often fail to fulfill our goals that brought us to Earth. It is far too easy, with free choice, to substitute lesser goals defined by power, greed, sex, self-centered ego, or drugs, for example. We may settle for immediate gratification or a trip on the wild side—even so there may be learning. Some of us are on a specific journey extending over several incarnations. Although some of us are seduced by all of the temptations around us, I believe that any incarnation is too important to waste!

Some may wonder, "How did God let this happen?" Recall that you and I have been given free will. That's an absolute on both sides of creation. We are all on a journey of spiritual growth involving many incarnations. After receiving a great deal of help, our lives are designed prior to incarnating. Our journey to fulfill an aspect of growth or responsibility may involve several incarnations. It is impossible to look at one incarnation and judge it from where we stand on the outside.

Unless we ask for direct help from our Spirit Guides, none will be forthcoming, except in matters of utmost seriousness. Remember to ask for help. Only your Spirit Guides can determine if their intercession is appropriate. Your difficulties may be very important to your soul. Remember to ask for guidance every day and always be grateful for life.

There are several ways for you to discover your mission if it is deemed appropriate that you receive this information (years of contemplation and thoughtful action would help prior to a request):

Have that knowledge given to you by your Spirit Guide or some
   Being from the Other Side.
Pray for the knowledge. If you receive an answer, fulfill it after
   giving it deep thought.
Meditate on your question. If you receive an answer, fulfill it after
   giving it deep thought.
Look at the pattern of your life and accentuate what you are most
   comfortable with.
Concentrate on what gives you inner joy.

Be at peace. The journey is to the Light! Lorraine provided me with a wonderful insight into the concept of mission that I related in the Postscript of our previous book. I'll repeat it since it clarifies so much.

September 25, 2002. 5:45 a.m.: Lorraine provided a fascinating bit of information. It absolutely amazed me. She said that we programmed her *passing back over* prior to our incarnating on Earth. We did this so that she would be able to provide insights to me from the Other Side unavailable to us while in a physical incarnation. This book was, then, a major part of our mission. We must have seen great importance for the book at that time. The importance was all about helping people. Her information from the Other Side places all understanding in a new and wonderful light. Recall, we have been given "free will" at all times (we are also responsible at all times). We could always have changed our minds when on Earth if we so wished. This also points out the great amount of work that our guides needed to do prior to our incarnation in order for it all to have a possibility of coming together.

I list some of the choices we made in our lifetime in order for a close and beautiful relationship to exist.

> We were in the same fifth grade in Public School 208 in Brooklyn, New York. This involved a move on Lorraine's part.
> We went "steady" at seventeen—then almost the equivalent of an engagement.
> We were married at twenty.
> We decided on a career of farming, instead of entering my family's business, to enable us to have a daily close relationship. (Without the learning experiences provided by the farm I never would have completed my doctorate at Cornell University.)
> When the farm had to be sold to allow space for a town industrial park, we decided on a teaching career instead of new opportunities in the family business.
> We selected early retirement from the University to again allow additional time together with a concentration on writing about spiritual matters.
> We had to live life together. Going separate ways, even when married, was out of the question.

Designing your mission and fulfilling it are vital parts of the process of spiritual maturity. It is important to yourself and those you interact with that this be done. I'm still in awe over Lorraine's latest information. An incarnation can be far more precise than I thought. It really is part of a vast puzzle that is beginning to make sense. Both sides of existence are closely intertwined. Life has much more meaning when we are open to all around us.

This confirmation leads me to the following conclusions:

We are now living in a universe but we do not come from the physical universe. Our creation and home are spiritual.

We have programmed our lives prior to incarnating. It's called our mission. We try to live a life of positive and responsible goals designed for maximum spiritual growth. (Again, we always have free will to choose our path. We also have the free will to deviate from our path and make horrible decisions.)

There is nothing to fear if we've followed our mission.

When you understand this you can live a life of complete joy and responsibility.

You can now fully realize that you are a *Child of the Universe* on a spiritual journey immersed in love. It is a love that you can experience and share.

We can make life, on both sides of the narrowing divide, our joy marching toward spiritual growth and maturity. It was designed that way!

We can accelerate spiritual maturity by overcoming difficulties, healing past actions, or living a life of joyful love.

CHAPTER 3

Transition in Time

You've passed over from the physical dimension to the spiritual plane. Your life on Earth has been a large part of your growth prior to entering the spiritual world. If you have ever thought about life after death or reincarnation, even a little, your first thoughts might be: "Hey! I'm not in pain. I'm not wiped out, I'm not dead! I'm alive! I'm awake! It really is true. I can begin again! I must be on my way to Heaven or whatever the Other Side is called!"

If you have been able to overcome or conquer confusion (this awesome event is bound to cause some confusion), the joy of awakening to your forever home is one of the great events in your existence. Can you think about what has just happened? You were on the threshold of the long sleep or perhaps the extermination of your consciousness, sometimes called death, when you realize that the opposite has just taken place. You are more awake now than you have ever been on Earth. Your greatest hope has been fulfilled.

You find yourself fading away from the physical scene and moving on, not quite sure where. Time may seem to pass as you move further from the physical world. Others appear in the distance and someone comes up close, perhaps your Spirit Guide (not an angel), whom you're beginning to recognize after having ignored him or her (the energy) during your entire sojourn on Earth. You immediately realize that your physical body was not aware of help or even that its soul was trying to offer advice. Now, as that soul, having discarded your physical ego, you recognize the error of your previous ways. It was so easy to just go along for the ride and not be concerned with anything more meaningful. You missed some wonderful opportunities for progress, the reason that you came down in the first place. Before you go further on your spiritual journey you visit your physical loved ones, if there is any interest. Some individuals, unfortunately, have none and that is so sad. You remember much that is painful, as you did not always live the life you now know you should have. You may even visit one or two places on Earth that you wanted to go to but could never find time.

As you move forward you pass above the Earth, close enough to appreciate beauty that had little interest for you before. How could it have been so? You see killing and devastation on a large scale, and you're astounded by the stupidity of those who see war as an answer to anything. You see horrific poverty that could be helped if anyone really cared. You never realized before how truly stupid many human actions are. We were not as civilized as we thought and you, like many people, gave little consideration to others or even your own inner self. You lived a superficial life entirely too self-centered. You may have wasted a great opportunity.

As you move onward you notice a rapid healing of your body, a shape that you will keep until you have made the complete transition or until you wish to be recognized in your proper energy form. Your guide helps you proceed, and you are witness to several planes of existence. Your guide takes you to a very large area where you are questioned briefly and then sent on your way to the group that you departed from prior to your life on Earth. Your thoughts fill with trepidation as you begin to become more aware of your accountability for lost opportunities. You know that you could have done better, you should have done better. There was so much more that you could easily have done. There was so much that you should never have done.

You pass many sights that are universal in manifestation but subjective in interpretation. Your level of attainment is the key to describing what you see. Your previous culture on Earth contributes to that subjectivity. If you are Jewish, you probably see and think with that outlook. If you are Christian, you see through that lens. Your previous attachments of whatever kind determine your early vision and understanding here. That was also true for your religious leaders on Earth. They spoke honestly but subjectively. All of that changes with time. For now, subjectivity rules. Fortunately, it will change into a clear vision of reality. Much of that will begin when you and others review your life with complete objectivity. The cobwebs will have dispersed. Reality will open your eyes.

You wish that your level of understanding was greater on Earth, but you never spoke up. You let the lesser desires lead and you made no comment. Again, too much time wasted in endless pursuits. You realize that how you viewed things on Earth is determining how you see them here, and that was not always commendable. It will soon change radically. But there is no hatred here and your understanding will blossom into harmony. You realize that there must be accountability, and you sincerely want to be accountable for your actions or omissions; they are essential for growth. They are essential for inner peace.

My son, Jesse Stoff, MD, in editing this chapter, volunteered generalizations that he has found true when he has been called in to be present with individuals approaching their time of passing. These are his suggestions for family members who can provide help for those nearing their time of crossing over. He suggests that these actions will help the dying person cross to the Light in peace and love.

- Notice that your loved one will spend more time in a deeper sleep. The body is preparing to let go.
- At times your loved one will be fully alert and will attempt to "bargain with the spiritual world" for causes good and true.
- Your loved one may see an entity fully consistent with his or her particular religious background, and will communicate very personal issues.
- Your loved one may become very psychic, and it is important that you be truthful in any discussions with them because any avoidance of truth will be immediately recognized.
- It is important that you help them resolve any interpersonal conflicts that may be remaining.
- Help them forgive others where there may have been conflict. Also, help them forgive themselves where appropriate.

- Ask about any unresolved issues and try to resolve them. Do your best to help them realize that there is no need for them to fear their passing. They are returning to a place of beauty, harmony, and love.

As I write this, it is now November 2003. I'm sitting in my home in Tucson, Arizona, thinking of the morning of April 17, 2001. I was then sitting in a chair next to Lorraine in her bed in a nursing home in Queens, New York City. I had taken her there after she suffered a stroke in our home in Ithaca, New York. I was hoping for rehabilitation since they had an excellent unit there. However, she began to suffer a series of strokes in the nursing home and now had lost the ability to speak. She nodded to my questions and listened as I read to her. Suddenly, as I was rubbing her arm she sat up, looked toward the foot of the bed, and said, "Chief Noblebird [her Spirit Guide whom she had known for decades], I love God and I want to go home. Please take me to the Other Side."

I found a napkin on her bedside table and began writing as soon as she began speaking. I'm sure that I wrote every word as she spoke (I've since framed the napkin to preserve the memory). Lorraine passed over almost twenty-four hours to the minute after speaking with Chief Noblebird. Joshua, my youngest son, who lived only an hour away, came to the nursing home after I called and asked him to come and tell Lorraine that it was OK to cross over now. She had fought long enough. We both said a teary farewell hours after her call to the Chief.

Now, two and a half years later, as I think of that day, I think that I ought to include in this chapter my memory of her passing over in order to put this all in context. I now asked Lorraine if she would contribute to this chapter as she had so often in the *Universal Kabbalah* book. She is standing behind me and dictating as I type this lengthy description.

There were feelings of release from a heavy bondage and pain. I experienced no confusion as I realized that I had left my body. I was finally wide awake! All that I experienced was a gentle pulling sensation. I floated upward slowly, with my eyes constantly on you. I was liberated from the pain and humiliation. I saw my body at rest. It had served me well but it was now time to move on without regrets. Knowing of the spiritual home, I had never feared death.

I saw you in tears but I knew that you would be relieved for me, knowing that my agony in the nursing home was finally ended. I had lost all of my ability to speak and I had been in constant pain. I appreciated your loving presence and your reading John Edward's book *One Last Time* to me. Your love made the end much easier for me. Thank you for not leaving me alone at such a crucial time. I recommend prayer and love for anyone in those final moments. It is so important for an easier passing.

We had frequently discussed reincarnation together, and I often began my presentations on spiritual matters with the statement that reincarnation is the only spiritual concept that I knew to be publicly verifiable. I received considerable support for that statement from priests, ministers, and others in the churches, but only privately. There was always the corollary that they couldn't support the concept publicly since it was not now church doctrine.

I'm thankful that we had spoken of reincarnation since I never suffered fright at all. Instead, I laughed several times as my homecoming went so smoothly. At all times in my journey home I felt surrounded by the love of God to a degree that I never was able to feel on Earth. It was a presence that I welcomed with joy in my heart. I believe that the beautiful light that was all about me was a manifestation of God's love that I could see and feel.

I was not afraid in my journey since I had experienced passing so many times before and we had talked about what might happen often during the past few weeks. It all seemed so familiar. I recalled how you prepared my father for his passing, and I know now that preparation should become standard in society. Without help there is only confusion unless you are aware of having done this many, many times. While preparation and spiritual growth should be a life-long process, it is essential in later years. Age in years should be accompanied by spiritual growth and the expansion of consciousness. I welcomed my transition as I hope all others can also.

I saw you grieving at my bedside in the nursing home for my physical loss yet happy that my journey home was now starting. Your constant love was a source of my inner strength. We all need that help but it is sad that few receive it. Prayer, by all who can take part, is so important at the end. It helps provide needed strength and comfort. I said the following prayer many times:

Dear Lord,
I know that I will soon start my journey home.
With all my heart I thank you for the joy and blessings of this life.
Please have Thy love always shine on those I leave behind. I love them.
I love you. Amen.

On Earth we prepare for events. Our passing at the appropriate time is the most important event of all, yet so few even think about being ready for this leap into pure spirituality. Knowing that we are all together in love and harmony here might have a powerful influence on the way people live their lives on Earth. I needed your love so badly and it was always there. Again, thank you, I love you. I love you.

The gentle pulling away from my tired body was a blessing. I looked around the room as I was a bit above the bed and I saw you crying. I kissed you on the cheek (you didn't notice) and I heard you telling me that you loved me. That was good since it showed that you knew that I was still with you in spirit and had survived my discarded body. I wished that others understood the realness of passing over, not only as a physical death but also as a wonderful spiritual awakening which can be more joyous than anything that you ever experienced on Earth.

I knew that I was on my way home, and I was excited and filled with joy at the event. I felt that we did well and that our plan would succeed. We would complete our mission from *both* sides of the divide. The light now seemed so bright but it never hurt my eyes. The light almost sparkled. It was incredibly beautiful in clarity and harmony. I had forgotten how beautiful light could be. I continued to feel the pulling and I moved quickly through endless sky and entered what appeared to be a darkened area, maybe a funnel or a tube, I'm not sure. I was quickly pulled or moved rapidly through it and I emerged onto another bright but soft light of endless space.

In advance, I seemed to know what was happening and I saw Chief Noblebird waiting for me. I knew that he would be there for me. The time in the nursing home was very hard on me, and the Chief now merged with me and gave me a quick healing charge to help me overcome my weakness. I appreciated it so much. I had really suffered, and even though I was now just soul and not body, I still needed a "quick fix." Those who have misspent their life on Earth will require much healing and long periods of contemplation followed by one or more incarnations of healing of self and others.

Loretta (my friend) and several others appeared with open, hugging arms. In order to help my adjustment they appeared as I remembered them. That changed when I was fully acclimated. I also remembered you saying that in my passing if I saw any strange sights they would simply be figments of my own imagination. Fortunately, everything that I saw was orderly and appropriate. I deeply appreciated the smoothness of it all.

In my journey home it was clear to me that there was no Gatekeeper. That was a surprise to me since I had expected one and had even thought who it might be. I don't know if there ever was one or if it was simply a story that has been passed down. It is common thought in some religions today. Perhaps it was meant to intimidate people and so add a dimension of fear.

Before continuing on I want to repeat that my passing was peaceful and I smiled the whole time since I recalled doing this so many times before. It was all happening as we expected, and I knew that our remaining task together would now proceed in a way that we had all carefully planned. Never did our Spirit Guides fail us. When you think of what they had coordinated to bring it all together you can begin to appreciate their talents.

I also recalled that I always knew that when I was on the Other Side it was real and eternal. Life on Earth is a passageway and a temporary site for learning through many physical experiences. (It takes much thought, experience, and love to grow to spiritual maturity. It's only when you realize the majesty of the goal that it all makes sense.) This Other Side is our permanent home, one that we all come back to.

Indeed, it is beautiful in every way here. Only here can the true meaning of community be fully comprehended. We live and study here in small communities that are part of larger communities. In order to fully appreciate the essential meaning of a community you have to witness a community on this side. Love, harmony, and helpfulness pervade all our thoughts and actions. Communities on Earth have a lot of growing up to do in order to earn that title. Heaven denotes such a beautiful reality, far more complex than we can ever imagine. All creation is diverse but always ONE. Our consciousness is everlasting and expanding. It is awesome, as the grand design is awesome! It is truly beyond our comprehension when in a physical body.

In your time I appeared with Loretta and Matthew Stoff [my nephew who had passed over twelve years before] the very next day at my funeral, but much had happened between my passing and my funeral even though it was only one day in your dimension. I believe that my long experience allowed me to move swiftly and I passed a "Gathering and Sending Area" for relative newcomers or for souls who might have messed up their past lives and needed immediate counseling. That area looked a lot like Grand Central Station on 42nd Street [New York City]. It was very large but very orderly. I smiled at how well organized it was. Atheists and those not understanding a continuing forever consciousness would also be very confused by all of this and would receive needed assistance. If they believed only in a physical existence they would be completely confused by present events. They might even think that they were still alive.

This similarity of both sides is maintained in order to make the transition as easy as possible. All of the things that you first encounter here look as though you are still on Earth. Because of this fact there are different reception areas, and you are sent to what would be familiar to you. Everything on this side was conceived first, and most things erected on Earth are mere copies created from memory, even though we never realize that. This continuity even follows when we return to our group or community. There we find things as they were on Earth. Houses and recreation areas abound. Again, this is to allow for a smoothness in transition. Some of what we see, we ourselves determine.

If individuals believed in an afterlife of hell and damnation, they would surely require counseling in this state of love and harmony. It is so difficult to remove the harsh view of this domain when it has been imposed on Earth for so long and so stridently. There are those who may be fearful as soon as they realize the pain that they had caused others by their violence, abuse, and narrowness. They would now fear punishment. That understanding will change after being here for some time as they grow quickly in insight. The growth in thought is very rapid for all, and this may also bring pain and distress as Earthly failures are understood by those who have just left an incarnation of little growth—an incarnation that may even have been harmful to themselves and others.

A positive incarnation may not be a happy incarnation, as we may have programmed ourselves into suffering as a learning experience. It may be a giant step forward. We are always responsible for our actions, and we will do whatever is needed here in order to overcome feelings that may have led to atrocious behavior. We will receive guidance during this process, which may require much time and may culminate in another incarnation.

One can never judge another while in an Earthly perspective. That is so important to understand. Your mission on Earth is to always care for, love, and respect, not judge. Judging and hating are great failures indicating little maturity. They will be overcome in future reincarnations.

Those individuals who are also filled with regret are those who have wasted their lives in boredom, apathy, greed, or struggles for power. When you agree to undertake your mission it is your responsibility to fulfill it. There is always so much to do in the short time on Earth. Individuals should fulfill what they decided they must do prior to coming down. Above all, it is so wrong to fail, through your own neglect, to complete a mission properly that only you can successfully complete. Others may have depended on you. On Earth you cannot see the big picture, but by acting in love for all and accepting responsibility for your actions, things should turn out as they were planned.

Our missions on Earth are such blessings. We always program for growth. We're encouraged to first correct and heal any wrongs that we are responsible for in a past incarnation. After that there is a life of love and growth on Earth that we can share with others. That seems to be a common failure in current times. Too often seduction by power, greed, drugs, sex, apathy, naked rationality, the self-centered ego, or material things gets priority. We no longer seek to uncover or even care why we came. That kind of incarnation is without value and may be hurtful, and may seriously set back your growth.

Let me remark here that your previous religion or religions have no status on this side. You will have selected one as a means for growth during an incarnation but may not always have used it that way. In addition, a self-centered ego on Earth may have been a difficult thing for some to overcome. It has always been so. You chose your body prior to incarnation. The ego may have been a challenge that you needed to overcome. Your actions, for good or bad, are the meaningful events in your stay on Earth. Remember, you always come in order to heal, to mature, and to be responsible.

After the initial meeting I went directly to my community or group setting. Eight of us were present and I was joyously welcomed. There is only love, caring, and responsibility here, and we are all so proud of each other. It was so good to be back. There was no discussion of my incarnation at this time. Such discussion was saved until I came back from my review.

Soon afterward the Chief and I went to an area where I was fully restored, and then we went to a second area of screens where notable events of my past life were reviewed with startling insights.

I tried to record what Lorraine shared. She knew that I was typing, ever so slowly, and she probably did not describe some events that she believed to be secondary in importance. That made it a lot easier on me. It's much more difficult to reach her these days, but I try because the meeting is so wonderful. Prayer, meditation, and early-morning awakenings continue to be the richest part of my life. Her presence and help in clarification are often part of my typing sessions.

After Lorraine passed over I gave some of her clothes to friends on condition that they think of her when viewing the clothing in the morning. I believe that our thinking and praying for those who have crossed over is a big help to their adjustment on the Other Side. When you love someone, you try to do anything and everything that can help. There's no reason for that love to stop with their passing. I prayed for my parents each day for fifteen years after they had passed. I only stopped when I felt that it was no longer needed. Additional giving of charity is also appropriate. Remember, most of all, that you are never alone. Lorraine's love for those she left behind is still there. Of that I'm sure. Why would she ever forget us? She still wants me to remarry and to continue to love her. Loving her was the easiest and most joyous thing that I ever did.

Again, let me repeat what I said in the *Universal Kabbalah* book. When I pray or meditate, I do so only as a Child of the Universe. I believe more strongly than ever that meditation is the strongest key to consciousness expansion. Prior to meditating I shed all other attachments since I strongly believe that what I see and what I hear can be influenced by my cultural and religious attachments. I seek an unadorned human truth with no ties to any institution. I also believe that meditation must be kept in balance with the four basics described in *Universal Kabbalah:*

· Study
· Prayer
· Good deeds and service to others
· Chanting and meditation (listening in a silence devoid of the self-centered ego)

I'm deeply grateful that Lorraine's passing over was accomplished in such a positive way. She deserves only goodness, and that was provided for her. I so look forward to remembering and knowing more of the Other Side. It's so good to share something of this importance with you and to kindle the knowledge that we all are Children of the most loving God.

CHAPTER 4

The Heroes Return

I briefly mentioned the greeting in the last chapter. I'll provide additional details here. Lorraine's first contact upon passing over was with Chief Noblebird, her primary Spirit Guide. After he escorted her preliminary entrance to the Other Side, she was greeted by Loretta, Matthew, her parents, and mine. They all looked the same as they had on Earth so as to make initial contact much easier and less confusing. This greeting was very brief, and she was returned to her community quickly for a more intensive joy and mingling.

All parties were very happy to be with her again in her community setting, and there was much laughter and deep-felt joy. A dear friend had returned from a very successful growth opportunity on Earth. There was much intertwining of light-energy as two entities or more gathered together for a grand welcome. Several left after the greeting since they were from different communities but wished to be present to unite with a cherished former friend or relative. Joy abounded. The meeting of Lorraine with her parents was a very special time. She and her mother, whom she loved dearly, now would be able to share time together because differences in personality had hindered their relationship on Earth. There was much hugging, and light energy surrounded all. Standing aside but always close at hand was the Chief, ever watchful, ever protective, ever helpful, ever caring. Greetings were mainly times for hugging by energy forms projecting human appearances. There was joy in the homecoming of a dear friend who was greatly admired. The Chief had organized much that occurred now and in the previous Earth-time. The Chief had also provided the times and places for the initial transition and homecoming.

Being greeted by someone close to us in the previous Earth-time does not always mean that they are in your small community. A community is usually composed of those of similar spiritual development. In order to make our greeting time as smooth and comfortable as possible, those who shared Lorraine's Earth-time also joined together for her welcome home.

Since Lorraine is a very advanced soul there was no confusion at that time, only a deep sense of relief on her part at having fulfilled all that she had set out to do on Earth. The critical part in the transmission of knowledge to me was still to come, and that future work was very much welcomed by her. What we had set out to do was on schedule.

If she had been an individual of lesser experience, her friends would have given her a tour of places that she would have forgotten, such as large communities, temples, the large library, leisure areas for the arts, and even study areas. There are vast places of seclusion used as needed by those with unsatisfactory Earth-time. Such a tour was unnecessary since she had all of these areas, and more, completely in mind. The only concern Lorraine had was why some of these details were missing from her Earthly religious education. Unfortunately, all older souls who cross over quickly realize that their religious education has been completely lacking in the fundamentals of what happens on the Other Side.

Sadly, one realizes on the Other Side how much is being continually distorted on Earth. That is so clear. Almost all people on Earth wear blinders and are missing the basic attitudes of caring, responsibility, brotherhood, and love for God and all of God's creations. The reasons for and understanding of reincarnations and a forever life are also absent for most. The sadness of that realization tempered the joy of coming home but intensified Lorraine's desire to get on with her mission responsibilities. It was time to again connect with me, but that would come after her incarnation was reviewed by the "Wise Ones" (a term used to denote respect and wisdom).

At this point I asked Lorraine directly if she would like to comment on this chapter of her greeting when she arrived home.

Sheldon's intuition and meditations of my arrival home are accurate. There is one point that I wish to elaborate on. Here I am surrounded by a peace and harmony impossible to achieve on Earth. I know that every entity I meet has my best interests always at heart. I know that I believe and act the same way. It is as if each entity and I are in the same loving, caring family. In fact, we are. So there is nothing held back. There are no hidden agendas. Imagine a place where all entities care for all other entities, and you can call it heaven. So it is. It is such a delight. We all are so fortunate and we always realize it. Thank you, dear God, thank you.

We all are truly blessed and filled with gratitude for the Most High. After my visit with the Wise Ones I will continue to work with you in order to complete our mission. It was a wonderful idea then. It is a wonderful idea now.

CHAPTER 5

Life Review and Counseling

Chief Noblebird accompanied me to our Life Review site for a full review of my incarnation on Earth. There is always some uncertainty when going for a session on a past-life review because there is much that we might have done that we didn't realize we should have done and—this is more common—some ways we have acted that were completely improper. The "sins of omission" are what can really cause you to think. When listening without an ego involvement you can gain so much more than if you tried to save face or shift the blame.

Now I know what I went to do; I can see the Life Reviews and listen to the Wise Ones who are the highest spiritual entities I ever encounter here. I really see all my actions in context. I also know that during and after these discussions it is I who will evaluate and I who will work on what needs changing. I also realize that past events cannot be undone but that a future incarnation may provide an opportunity to help heal any wrongs that require correction. Thus, I grow on both sides of the divide. Spiritual maturity is all about growth in sensitivity, awareness, and being at one with the process. I am no longer looking in. In reality, I become aware that I am an actively working part of the Cosmos.

You might call it Cosmic Consciousness.

Together, the Chief and I entered a large structure and proceeded to enter a smaller area within which were housed seven screens. The one in the center seemed to be about 5' x 7'. The three on each side were about 3' x 5'. In front of the center screen was a table and chairs. As we stood facing the center screen, with the Chief a few paces behind me, five Wise Ones [souls] entered the area and took their seats They all appeared old and wore capes, both perhaps for effect. There was no anger or fright on my part. As I said, I was a bit anxious but completely certain that the Wise Ones had my best interests at heart. That was an important concept to fully accept.

Views of my past life began to flash on all of the screens, and the center screen, the largest, showed the most relevant episodes. As the views appeared on each screen the Wise One, seated in the center, spoke kindly to me. The discussions were brief at this time so that I could view the scenes carefully. The Wise One mainly pointed out the core of each scene. I saw you staring at me in the fifth grade when you were the class monitor. I never realized that you looked at me that way. I always thought that it was only me who noticed you. We should have spoken more—even the Wise One pointed this out. The sooner that we were close, the sooner our mission could begin in earnest. We were beginning then but not acting together. It was possible then to start building our future. It waited until our senior year in high school and it blossomed after graduation.

Our contact at that point in time was immediate and awakening. We understood that we would always be together in this venture. The views showed our joy and commitment. They even showed me studying for a test one evening and you reading while seated in a chair in my room. When you drove home I heard you say, 'What a great night.' That was so good to hear since we didn't say twenty words to each other all night. Our vibrations must have made up for our inactivity. I was so glad to hear your words since I had concentrated on my studies and knew that I ignored you. Now I know that we were both active spiritually, and that's the best kind of action.

The Wise One pointed out several times that in making decisions we generally came from two different directions, me artistically (since I am an artist), you pragmatically and philosophically. He thought that the final answer was arrived at properly and was always moving in the appropriate direction. That was so important and the views showed it all. He was also glad to see that we made our decisions on the basis of what we together thought was right, and we did not give financial considerations much weight. When I looked at the scenes I realized that much of what we did was of an intuitive nature. Even though we talked about the details, we seemed to make the final choice from the heart.

The Wise One went to my college years and pointed out how I selected my first major by listening to my dad, who wanted me to take a scientific orientation. Since I wanted to teach children my heart told me that it was the wrong choice. As a chocolate scientist he thought that he was doing the best for me, but he didn't consider my heart. I should have stood up for myself because I was acting from a much deeper level. I should have acted in love for what should have been my first choice. I finally straightened it out in my second year but I wasted valuable time. The Wise One mentioned the need for my soul to always be considered and acted upon. He was glad that you and I understood that and it constantly guided us. I learned a great deal from that mistake, and future decisions went much better. It was so important to keep on learning from events. Right decisions are an important part of our growth. If you or I had chosen wrongly in this incarnation, our mission would have failed in spite of all the previous work of our guides.

The Wise One said that there were six crucial decisions that we had to make in order for me and for us to successfully complete our mission. As he described them the screens were filled with views of them. This was the most emotional part of my review, and the Wise One emphasized that I passed them all. I was completely overwhelmed with joy and gratitude.

1. We married at age twenty. This was no real decision for me since it was so obvious, but my friends thought that marrying at such an early age to a college student was a mistake. They didn't understand that we were meant for each other. The Wise One said that one reason for our coming in the current time was to demonstrate what a truly happy marriage was. Such demonstrations are taking place by many couples who volunteered on the Other Side, since the Other Side is very unhappy with our marriage failures on Earth. There is too much self-centeredness in people. People seem to have no idea of how to live a life of significance, growth, and love. It is so important to care for each other and to be responsible for all that we say and do.

2. We decided on a farm life so that we would be together and be close to our children. You had some family opposition but you left New York

University pre-law and entered Long Island Ag and Tech. We both wanted you to be a farmer and not a lawyer. It was a necessary decision, and we passed that hurdle. If we had based the decision on income and not our hearts, it would have changed our lives and aborted our mission.

3. We decided on beginning our family at a time when farming did not provide the kind of income that would make the decision an easy one. Two wonderful souls joined us and I'm grateful for their choice. We couldn't have had finer children. In looking back at their choices I believe that it was right for them and right for us. Our prayers before conception must have helped their decision.

4. Farming gave you the ability to persevere when events were difficult. After we sold our farm because of the town's decision to have an Industrial Park on our land and the land adjacent to us, you applied to Cornell University and were accepted in the program to teach agriculture. We went to Cornell and you met with your advisor. Again we had to make a major decision: return to the family wholesale shoe business and immediate income, or go to Cornell as a student. You were wavering since you knew that it would be difficult for our family. I strongly supported Cornell. Again, money never stood in the way. You made the final choice and we went to Cornell. Our mission was still on the correct path.

5. After you graduated from Cornell you taught Agricultural Science very successfully at Schoharie High School. Your success was equaled by the joy of living in a wonderful farming community. When you received a telephone call asking you to return to Cornell as a graduate assistant to work on your doctorate, there was another major decision to make. We were happy in this beautiful farming community but you felt that there were concepts in philosophy that you wanted to explore that were being ignored ("freedom, religion," etc.). Again, the choice was between current income and stability, and your belief that we had to move forward. This was your choice and I did not stand in the way.

Again, it was the right choice. The salary of a graduate assistant was small and with two children it was difficult, but it was a necessity. You acted from your intuition and I fully supported the move. We proved to be a wonderful team.

6. Upon graduation you accepted a position at Adelphi University on Long Island, which allowed you to also study with your rebbe. [A rebbe is an ordained rabbi who is also a spiritual master.] You were asked to remain at Cornell, a more prestigious university, but your choice of Adelphi was the right one, and I fully supported it. You studied with your rebbe for three years and we, together, continued our spiritual studies all our lives. I fully honored our decision, made prior to incarnating, to help with our book, *Universal Kabbalah: Dawn of a New Consciousness.*

Passing over was a difficult decision to make since we were so happy together. If you remember, I even told our relatives and friends that you were "Saint Sheldon" because you cared for me so well during my illness. I also stressed to them that you should remarry. Leaving you was so hard, but again, a necessity if we were to complete our mission. It was so important to let my soul influence my physical decisions at these critical times and not make the choice on the basis of income or life stability. We simply had a bigger issue in our life. We had to complete what we came for.

When the review was complete the Wise One said that I had done well so far but that my mission was yet to end. He said that all that was done had led me to this very important part of my commitment. Because of our being love-bound and your decades of meditation, he thought that you would be receptive to my offerings. I left the area filled with joy, and the Chief had a long talk with me about the incarnation and how I might go about helping with the book. Your part, as well, would be a solitary effort requiring much meditation.

This sort of help from here to the Earth is far more common than people think. It is a basic part of life for people who are open to receive.

As you write now you know that the effort was successful and that a fine, very helpful book resulted, *Universal Kabbalah: Dawn of a New Consciousness.*

The Life Review was so helpful and I learned a great deal. The Chief also helped after the review in clarifying my whole progression on Earth. Once I let faulty advice guide my actions in college. I learned from that experience and never made that mistake again. To make decisions from my inner Being, my spark, my soul, my consciousness, is the wisest course of action always, at all times! It does require humility and the ability to listen. This past incarnation was and is so valuable for my spiritual maturity.

The Chief pointed out that seeing the *purity of my soul* was the strongest part of my review. It was shining for all to see and was my greatest asset. He smiled broadly and was so pleased with my incarnation. I had succeeded in strengthening my ability to communicate with the body I was living in. This was also one of my tasks this time. It took me several incarnations to develop my ability to consistently do so. I had to learn to be assertive in a loving, caring manner with the body that I had chosen for the incarnation.

After this discussion of the review the Chief took me to the Hall where the Akashic [past life] Records are kept in order to review several past lives so that I could see how much my ability to communicate with my body had progressed. The Hall is so inspiring and is such a magnificent structure. I almost felt that I was entering a revered old church or synagogue. One of the Keepers brought out my records on a parchment scroll, and as we studied them they seemed so vivid, so alive. Studying on Earth was never like this. My progress was clear and I could easily witness the positive growth. Reviews and lessons here include images and are always presented in a loving, involved way. They use extremely powerful ways of communicating.

It is important to clarify the outcome of a Life Review for any who have caused harm or suffering or have committed suicide. They will be reminded of this very graphically. They have *wasted* a very precious life on Earth! Their incarnation was a step backward. *They* will want and need to experience all the pain and suffering that they have caused. It will be their choice as a way of overcoming the attitudes that allowed that action to occur. They will even choose future incarnations in order to continue to grow and to help right some of the wrongs they committed. It will be a difficult road to follow but it is one that they will wish to follow. Their faulty actions will be regretted and they will want to atone and correct.

We are accountable on the Other Side for our actions on Earth. Persons who have caused harm will not be at ease until they are able to right the wrongs that they have acted out. It is so important to recognize that *no one here punishes another.* All of us correct our harmful actions because we are responsible and we wish to correct them. We wish to be accountable. In closeness to the eternal One it could be no other way. Though even here we can demur from growth choices if we so wish. It does occasionally happen. We have free will. We can tread water if we want to.

On Earth, the love-force of the Indwelling Presence is usually shielded so as not to interfere with our decisions and actions. This allows us to make choices without the felt Presence and gives us a greater opportunity and responsibility for actions, good or bad, which may even deviate from our selected mission. We always have free will. We are always responsible and our actions are always reviewed.

Here, we may feel the Oneness at all times, and we try to reflect that love and goodness. A high standard is set and we seek our growth toward the eternal One.

CHAPTER 6

A Period of Reflection

There was much to think about after my past-life review. The Chief and I had a detailed conversation after the review and he emphasized three areas that I should dwell on, even though my review was very positive. He felt that there were areas that I could pursue since I was open to the truth and lived in the truth. That is an essential for all of life on both sides. I appreciated his assessment.

There is always room for growth. We are always in a learning modality, both here and in an Earthly incarnation. That seems reasonable since we have such a long road to travel toward our goal. When you look at it this way you realize the joy in learning, the blessing of growth. It is all movement toward the eternal One. No one could ask for more. As you move forward you are opened to and encompassed more and more by the abundance of love. When you finally realize that connection you seek out opportunities for learning, for love, for service.

I list the three areas that the Chief asked me to dwell on in seclusion and then later in discussion with friends:

Free choice
Serving
Intimate relationships

After a considerable time of serious but so very insightful contemplation on a hilltop setting similar to that which we had in Ithaca, additional conversation with my friends, and then help from the Chief, I arrived at the following conclusions, all supported and agreed upon by the Chief.

FREE CHOICE

The essence of a proper choice is one made with love, passion, caring, and affection for the outcome. There is absolutely no thought of self in the process. There is no thought of gain in the process. There is only the desire to do good with warm love and joy in your heart for all of God's creations. Suggestions from others made to you requesting decisions based on hatred, monetary gain, or increased power or lust can easily dissuade you from your selected mission. Remember, your mission is one of healing for growth. You are on Earth on a mission of spiritual growth. There is no need for immediate self-gratification; that will only bring harm to your incarnation. Your incarnation on Earth is only for a fleeting second in time. Accomplish it as you intended to when you could see more clearly from the Other Side. *Choose the eternal* rather than the momentary, however flashy and satisfying it might appear. The immediate gain for pleasure may bring long-term suffering.

In making choices we should act from love not fear. If we are afraid of doing evil, that reason alone is insufficient. We act out of love as a positive affirmation of our love for God. Fear is a faulty motivator with no depth. It states that we really do not know the difference between right and wrong. It demonstrates immaturity. We must teach the physical body to be open to the difference in vibrations between noble and immature choices. We must be more forceful in explaining our decisions to the physical brain. We should work very hard to prevent self-centered bias from dominating physical choices. The key words are love for the action. We can learn so much in a physical incarnation. It is the true test of what we work for and what we believe.

SERVING

Since we are all connected to God as our spiritual parent and we all have a soul connection to God at all times, we are all related. This is an everlasting truth to guide all our actions. It is as undeniable as the morning dew. By serving and helping each other we make actual the reality that we are all *Children of God*. We love and serve God by serving all of God's creations—be it nature, fellow creatures, or the spiritual domain.

Thus, service to and for others is one of the greatest pleasures that we can attain. People on Earth rarely understand this reality. Service to all is a good place to begin spiritual growth. This lesson ought to be mandatory for all those in power in business or government. When we serve others we serve God, for the spark of God is within everything and everyone! A life of service is a wonderful calling. By serving in any of many capacities we are living a life of dedication to the eternal One. It is an incarnation devoid of the self-centered ego and one in which we gladly offer ourselves to humankind on a daily basis. Begin by being helpful. Let us finally realize that when we help another we also help ourselves grow spiritually.

In a real sense by living a life of service, and it certainly may be in a happy marriage, a life of business, a life as a professional, a life as a garbage collector, or even a life in politics, service to all in an I–Thou capacity is a genuine description of a noble life. It is a major commitment prior to incarnation. It should remain so when we get to Earth. It is genuine relationship to the eternal One. It is a part of the each and the all.

In my review it was clear to me from the scenes and from the Wise Ones' discussion that service had been an important part of my life, and now I am very grateful that it had been so. A life without continuous service to all is an exercise of the self-centered ego. A life of service for all is a life of love and joy, and it is a life of love for God. The Jewish tradition of mitzvah, doing a good deed, sums up this basic condition of life. It is one of our four basic, *daily* tasks, previously described [study, prayer, good deeds, and chanting and meditation].

To serve all of God's creations, living beings and material substance alike, is the most wonderful of joys! As we mature, so will others mature. We are candles of light for each other. Service to others is always service to God. There is no higher or nobler task.

INTIMATE RELATIONSHIPS

A thorough understanding of an intimate relationship begins with friendship, and it can quickly mature with your understanding of what Martin Buber called an *I–Thou* relationship of respect and caring and even love, in contrast to the more commonly used Earthly *I–It relationship*. In an I–It relationship we may intellectualize, we may control, we may use selfishly, we may manipulate, yet we never intimately encounter the other. It is a life without true partnership, a life without love, a life without growth or maturity. It is using others as a thing. Such a life is hardly worth living. Now, it sometimes seems necessary in a large industrial nation to act in an I–It manner, but it is always a very distorted way of life. It will change as we mature. Life requires a balance of the I–Thou relationship in *every corner* of our existence. A full I–Thou encounter always includes the It in background. It is always full and comprehensive.

In sharp contrast to the ego-self-centered life is the I–Thou relationship of caring, of compassion, of complete and absolute responsibility, of loving into oneness. It is our charge and our challenge. Living a balanced relationship on Earth will lead us to our ultimate relationship with the eternal One. The first step leads inevitably to the final step. Taking the first step is the most difficult. It requires love and commitment but is saturated with joy and wonder. You have opened a door and there is no return. You have pierced the darkness and you are forever bathed in light. Your consciousness has opened to the universe. Do not be shy about this commitment. It is why you are here. Think small and begin now precisely where you are at every moment. Every moment and action is to be cherished.

One thought stood out when my solitary review was completed. All three categories are intertwined. You choose wisely and you act from your spiritual core that brings you into a helping, serving relationship with all of creation. You finally understand that only in true loving relationships with others are you acting from your authentic Being, your soul. Know also that it is most important in what you bring to a relationship. If you have been able to act independently in a balanced way you will bring much to any relationship. In entering into a relationship you should not be running away from negativity. You should be moving forward to completion.

Your upper soul has always remained on this side, even when you incarnated.

Sheldon's note. There are five parts to the soul, labeled in Kabbalah:

- Yehidah
- Chayah (these two upper parts always remain attached to God)
- Neshamah
- Ruach
- Nefesh (these three parts incarnate with us on Earth)

The soul always remains in relationship with the eternal One. This is the ultimate relationship to which all others will lead. Understanding this, when in an incarnation, will lead to a world-wide community of humankind on Earth, our ultimate human relationship. Joy and peace will be the core of human existence.

CHAPTER 7

Schooling with
Its Seven Divisions

L orraine described this section to me, and a different type style is used where I recorded her communications word for word. I'm always in awe of what she sends. It never occurred to me that there might be schooling on the Other Side. Reading her descriptions, it now makes perfect sense. It could be no other way.

Schooling on the Other Side is very different from that which we experienced on Earth. It always involves active subjects who seem to come alive *[I don't really understand Lorraine's communication about active subjects or living presentations. Perhaps it comes through that part of our consciousness which is more dreamlike—holographic, so to speak. —SS]* or are part of a performance for the benefit of fellow souls. Discussions always follow, and all becomes very attuned to vibrations that give us feelings of right and wrong. These feelings may be of a sun rising (good) or the moon setting (bad). At times, guides join in and at other times they allow the souls themselves to discuss issues at great length. These discussions are very much welcomed, as all souls learn so much from each other. Souls have the insight, and the discussions bring it out. Most souls are always trying to improve, and all in my community fit into that category. Absolute truth is part of our environment. Life is so much more pleasant when there is no one to doubt. I always look forward to such learning time.

There are ways here in which we experience the essence of each level listed below. There are subtle yet powerful vibrations attached to everything that is done. Here, two energies, soul-mates if possible, merge with each other saying the words of the appropriate level that they are studying. They do this several times and try to project the feeling that they have been taught. They can then experience the level from the "inside." They hold this position for what would be, in your dimension, about twenty minutes though often held much longer. This action gives you an inner understanding of the concept at hand in a way that is impossible to duplicate. You experienced this merging with me after I crossed over, and you needed reassurance that I was still there for you. I showered you with PEACE and you responded very well. All learning here is so much more meaningful than that experienced on Earth, where it is often simply cerebral. Such learning has little substance or vitality and needs to be improved upon.

When entities finally arrive at Level One they are asked to experience Oneness. I do not have the ability to describe that experience since it is so overwhelming. Needless to say, I welcome the opportunity to share it with you when you come home. It will be our greatest joy!

On Earth, people should begin to understand this merging process if they are of sufficient maturity. The two parties of a love-bound marriage can hold each other, wearing no clothes. They will then softly repeat a concept that they are trying to experience. Words like PEACE, LOVE, FREEDOM, etc., can serve as a beginning. Allow twenty minutes of receptivity. If continued over a period of daily practice, much will be gained by the experience. People will begin to know from the "inside." They will begin to awaken.

What Lorraine has transmitted to me is what I try to communicate to readers. Some messages are lengthy, some very brief. Regardless of length, the intuitions and communications are as accurate as I can make them. I do try very hard to fulfill the charge that I have accepted. I relate the lessons to be learned from the presentations and discussions. All that I write about is reviewed and accepted by Lorraine. As mentioned, when she offers a direct contribution, it will be distinguished here by a different type style.

It took a great deal of meditation for me to finalize the divisions or levels of education on the Other Side into seven separate learning areas. Lorraine had to step in and help and share with me the knowledge that she attended level two in the past, one below the top. All who knew her realized that she is in an advanced state, and she confirmed it now without hoopla. It is simply a fact of her being. In addition, it took even more time to fill in the curriculum in each category because they aren't exotic in any way. They're just potent enough to change our world. When the curricula were complete I understood the ancient maxim:

As Above,
So Below.
As Below,
So Above.

These seven categories are broad dimensions of knowledge and awareness that are needed on Earth, but they are studied here with a much deeper quality. This awareness must come into life on Earth. The categories are a level beyond our normal perception. I should have realized this from the beginning. When something is shown to you, only then do you realize that you should have known it all along. It's now so obvious.

For most people on Earth, life is lived in a very superficial way. It's all surface, all foreground, all appearance. Many talk about spirituality but don't practice it, don't live it, refuse to try to understand it. So many take the easy way out by continuing a life of fundamentalism—a narrow, distorted creed of favoritism where no thinking is required—or they live a life of apathy and ignorance. Too few welcome a life of seeking and spiritually maturing. Valuable time is wasted as whole incarnations may be seduced by violence and hatred, and thus, suffering may become a way of life.

On this Side the spiritual foundations are always explained in depth in significant encounters at each learning level. The goal is to take this knowledge back to Earth so that it all becomes part of our Being, regardless of circumstances. It's easy to think that you know something. It's far more difficult to live it and to be fully at one with it. That's what Earth life should be all about, to be at one with knowledge, action, and experience. Only then have you really known it. It has become part of your Being. Only then can you live in harmony and spiritually mature.

Level 7: Helpfulness (The Beginning)
Level 6: Gratitude and Freedom of Thought
Level 5: Charity and Forgiveness
Level 4: Be Open to the New (Even Here); Silence is Golden
Level 3: The Grandeur of a Love-Filled Marriage
Level 2: Love, Knowledge, Compassion, Truth, and Responsibility
Level 1: Oneness (The Goal)

LEVEL 7. HELPFULNESS *(THE BEGINNING)*

Knowing here that we truly are brothers and sisters, that we are each souls created by the eternal One, that we are all linked together in being firmly attached to God, we realize that by helping another we are helping a Child of God. *Change yourself* and you may change others. It is also helping ourselves because we are truly joined together for all time. It is simply one finger helping another on a giant hand. We don't harm our thumb because it isn't as long as our middle finger. So why harm our brother because he looks different or thinks in a different way? Such thoughts of hatred are only for the bigot. To harm another indicates a loss of rationality and humanity, other than when the act is committed in self-protection *(Thou shall not kill)*. All fingers on your hand join together to perform together. The same should be true of all souls, of all humans. Helpfulness is a sign of community, our goal and home.

Helpfulness also implies a higher step in consciousness. It implies that we always stand in a state of consciousness that recognizes the binds that lash all of us together, at all times, in all places. There are no times that the relationship is cast asunder. We live it, always. There are no excuses, no lapses of responsibility. We are always our brother's keeper. We are to make each moment holy. That action begins with each individual acting in a noble manner, showing kindness to all people and all things; always being helpful to those in need, our brothers and sisters.

"If not now, when?
If not you, who?"
—HILLEL

Living in the "now" of eternity makes each moment come alive. When there is caring and love, always at the core of every moment of existence, there is always binding, there is always one helping and caring for the other. *This includes you and me.* Loving the other is, at all times, loving our Creator in the most practical of ways. You cannot love the eternal One without loving God's creations. It is an impossibility! Helping and loving, for one begets the other, are our ways of living. There are no small deeds. No large deeds, only caring, helpful, loving, deeds.

This way of life is the first and perhaps most important step on the path of spiritual growth. There is no way in which *helping others* should be avoided. There is no way in which it should be trampled on. The small essential deed performed on a daily basis is some of what you will see in your Life Review. It is *that* important. It is so important as a step on the path that it may take many incarnations to achieve. Simply be helpful with no thought of any return. Do you request a return for loving God, or is love of God a matter of your essential Being?

LEVEL 6. GRATITUDE AND FREEDOM OF THOUGHT

Gratitude

I find it unfortunate that religious leaders rarely mention our pervasive lack of feelings of loving gratitude for the eternal One. Certainly the One who has given us a consciousness to expand and total free choice of thought deserves a depth of gratitude impossible to even describe. For one moment think of where you would be without those gifts. You would be non-existent! You would never have been born. You would never have had the opportunities to progress toward God in a way that

you would be comfortable with. You would never have had the opportunities to redress wrongs that you have committed or to experience
love or to see or hear beauty. You would never have had the opportunity to experience life, to have had a single thought, to breathe fresh air
or view a magnificent sunset. You would never have had the opportunity to help others, to care for others. You would never have felt love
and gratitude for a parent, a spouse, a child, or even a puppy. You
would have missed the opportunities to love God and all of God's creations. There is no greater love than that! You would never have been!
The light in your eyes would never have been a thing of beauty.

The eternal One created your soul so that you could experience and
learn from all of the wonderful thoughts that I listed above. Most
blessed of all, the upper portion of your soul is always attached to God,
and the lower portions may always mature toward God. You have an
experience in eternity as a never-to-vanish soul, capable of loving God
and all of God's creations, always. You can even be a co-creator with
the eternal One by your heart-felt love. There is no way to fully repay
the bounties heaped upon us, but we can begin by loving and helping
all, by being compassionate to *all,* by living a life of joy, gratitude, and
responsibility for the eternal One's constant gifts. A life of gratitude
keeps us focused on the bounties of God rather than on our meager
accomplishments, however noteworthy. These accomplishments may
seem to be something that we inwardly crave for all the "right" reasons.
As we evaluate them quietly, do we love and act without reserve for all
of God's creations? Are we filled with gratitude for the One who always
walks by our side? Does the force of this gratitude pervade our daily
thinking and praying? Do we constantly "know" that without God's
constant love we would not be here to even offer our prayers of gratitude? We would not Be without the eternal One's love! We could not
make our life holy without gratitude for our creation and the creation of
others and the creation of the universe.

Always, at all times, gratitude for the eternal One and the eternal One's creations should be at the core of our thoughts and prayers.

Freedom of Thought

[For a philosophical statement of the concept of freedom, read my chapter on Freedom found in *Universal Kabbalah*. In essence, freedom must be experienced in order to be fully understood. It is not intellectual action; rather it is loving action from your soul. You will or have recognized the difference. —SS]

As the eternal One loves all and has no favorites, you, born in the image of the eternal One, should also act without favoritism, acting in love for the deed which is truly action guided by your soul. Your free will should lead you to the nobility of freedom, to the awakening of your soul, your authentic self. Soul action is loving action, action in freedom.

LEVEL 5. CHARITY AND FORGIVENESS

Charity

We all know in our souls that everything comes directly from the eternal One. The problem is in our soul communicating that information to our physical body, and having the body react to the information in a meaningful way. The soul (consciousness, the spark) understands the unity of all persons and understands that part of its mission in coming to Earth is to awaken the body to love God and all the children of God. With that knowledge the role of charity in the lives of each of us becomes clear. Yes, we are always our brother's keeper even when we don't care for the actions of our brother! Our brother or sister always has the spark within and we are not to judge.

"Judge not that you not be judged."
—MATTHEW 7:1

Prior to incarnating, you programmed yourself to be in the position that you now hold. You left this Side with the knowledge that all is God's! All are God's Children. The next step is easy when you are awake to the connection. How dare you judge those who may have pro-grammed a harder scenario than that which you chose? The two fit together. Share with those in need what you temporarily possess. Acknowledge their spark by treating all Children of God with the respect due each of us. Help your brothers when you are able to. Remember that their spiritual parent is the same as your spiritual parent!

You can't judge, but there is the possibility that those in need chose their position to learn humility by receiving help from you at this time, and that you chose this time to learn caring, love, and responsibility.

Since all our bounties are temporary gifts of the eternal One, it seems reasonable that sharing and the acknowledgement of unity are part of prudent spiritual acknowledgement. Gifts were clearly not given to us to be hoarded by those who are trying to overcome greed. Giving is then a mutually rewarding act, a mutual act of learning and compas-sion. Both parties to "giving" may be testing themselves. Give with caring. Receive with gratitude.

In a previous incarnation you may have placed yourself as the receiver of charity as a powerful learning experience in humility. Now, you may be in the opposite position in order to learn to share and to be responsible. You may learn to awaken to the bond among all Children of God. Never doubt the complexities of life; therefore live with love and responsibility because that is at your core, perhaps well hidden, but ready to awaken when you are willing to listen. While you are learning to share, also remember to feel appreciation and gratitude for what you now hold dear. The opportunities for learning never cease as long as you are on Earth.

Your free recognition of your obligations to give in charity is an open recognition of the bond among us all. We are all souls in the dance of life, and we have obligations in knowing of these bonds. You don't give because you just "like" another. *You share because we are all Children of God.*

In the clear choice between "selfishness" and "sharing," which do you choose? Which do you choose knowing in your soul that you are forever bound to your neighbor? Which do you choose in full acceptance of an I–Thou relationship to your fellow dance partners? The music never stops. The commitment plays on as you dance through life.

When you choose to share with other Children of God, you are aware that giving is a necessary stepping stone as you continuously build your relationship with the eternal One. It is mutual, and sharing is part of your opportunity and responsibility to do your part. Since we are all bound together, in giving to others you are also giving to yourself. Giving to others and loving God are all part of a loving continuum. The bonds that hold us together are complex and engulfing. Charity allows us to make them more obvious and current.

Give what is temporarily yours to those who are permanently your brothers and sisters and also permanently Children of God.

Forgiveness

This Other Side, commonly called Heaven, is a place of joy, harmony, and unconditional love for most. Those who have harmed themselves by a misspent incarnation are given ample opportunity in which to improve their condition, and they will take all measures to do so, even at the cost of considerable time and pain. In their Life Review there will be sufficient counseling to aid in their progress, but when witnessing their Life Review they will immediately see the error of their ways and will actively seek methods of correction. Whatever needs to be done they will gladly do, for their own regrets of a substandard life will be immediate and severe in this place where love prevails. If you are at fault you know it immediately when viewing your transgressions, and your errors will be pointed out in caring, kindly ways by advanced souls who wish only to help.

Recall, here there is no punishment of one soul by another. There is no hatred or judgment of another, so there need be no forgiveness of another. It is never an issue. When there is unconditional love for all, forgiveness never becomes an issue here. When you are aware of the close relationship that we all have with the eternal One, you seek only to help those who have had a poor incarnation. You know that that soul in Life Review is horrified at their life performance and needs help, not hatred. You know that they, in their contriteness, will do whatever it takes to cleanse their soul, regardless of how long it takes or what efforts will be necessary.

Here, you always feel the pain that you have inflicted upon others since you are always bound to all others both here and on Earth. You have no wish to avoid whatever it takes since your remorse is considerable. You offer no excuses for your past life; you want only to atone and improve yourself so that it doesn't happen again. You want desperately to help and heal those whom you have harmed. Here, you never lose your sense of responsibility and you have profound regret for your errors. Healing yourself and helping others is your chief concern. It is a concern you will want to take back to Earth, along with your sense of responsibility.

Since we are all bound together, it is easy to see that the pain that an individual has caused others will now cause that individual to want to experience that pain as a way of burning out the attitude that allowed the transgression. That individual will also spend considerable time in solitary contemplation in an endeavor to overcome past failures. The individual now knows that it allowed its physical body to act poorly, and it must now understand why it allowed that behavior to occur. When the individual and those guiding it have observed full improvement here, only then may it be permitted to correct past misdeeds by subsequent incarnations.

The individual's horrendous acts on Earth have also scarred the soul, and only by replacing that hatred with love can a soul heal itself. Yes! The lower three parts of the soul can be harmed by a wicked incarnation. All of this healing may take eons of time, but here, in the spiritual domain, you are never rushed into an incomplete healing. Since we are always responsible, we urgently want a full healing to occur.

In this place of love and harmony your guides and Wise Ones have never felt anger toward any individual. There is only compassion for all, victim and doer alike. Of this you are always sure and completely open to help, but there is always the realization that it must finally come from within. Anger must be replaced by love, callousness by caring, manipulation of others by compassion and bonding.

Forgiveness by others is not an issue here when we know that we all live by God's grace and that we are all related. The issue at hand is healing, not vengeance! Help, not retaliation! So it must be on Earth. It is a lesson that we all want to bring with us when we return to Earth. Gandhi showed the way when he was shot. He, critically wounded, immediately offered forgiveness. He never felt hatred. As a Child of God there is no room for hatred. There is only healing and brotherhood. Earth is the proper place to forgive self and others for any inequities that have been caused. The ability to forgive self and others is a step up on the ladder. It should lead to an increased awareness of our actions. Only forgiveness, of self and others, can open the heart that hatred has closed. Yes, it will even help you to sleep better at night.

LEVEL 4. BE OPEN TO THE NEW, EVEN HERE; SILENCE IS GOLDEN

Open to the New

To be *Open to the New* in an Earth incarnation is to pierce the appearance and to behold the essence of that which you perceive. There should always be the understanding that there is always the spark of God in all Beings and in all creation. That simply means that all encounters are to be conducted with respect and caring, even the smallest.

If you must take down a tree or put down an animal, ask for forgiveness and permission to do so, and be sure that there is no other way of handling the situation. Always treat the other carefully and respectfully. Keep in mind that we are all connected, even inanimate objects. The connection to the living—humans, animals, and nature—is even closer. Everything is a creation of the eternal One. All is holy. All encounters are to be treated as holy encounters since everything and every one is a loving gift from God!

Our use of people and nature as "things" is so prevalent on Earth. Wars, poverty, greed, and the misuse of nature are the chief culprits. *[The only way that I can understand what Lorraine is saying here is to go to my familiar frame of reference from my discourses with Martin Buber regarding the distinction between I-It (a thing) and I-Thou (a respected entity). Remember that Saint Francis was fond of saying "Brother Sun, Sister Moon." —ST]* Our encounters must involve higher standards. Violence against humans and nature must cease, and governments must find peaceful ways of handling disputes. Would we have it any other way in a society that considers itself civilized? It is so clear that our temporary home, the Earth, must be treated far more kindly. At present, for many, there is no foresight, no respect.

Behold all people as "Thou" and the relationship of the encounter changes as much for you as for the other. It will not change until people change. Behold nature as "Thou" and your spiritual growth continues to expand and nature thrives. You are beginning to understand reality! You are beginning to be open to the truth.

When each of us and all of nature become a "Thou," the world will change and we will understand the blessings of the Light. Harmony, respect, and caring have been brought down from the Other Side and now will engulf our planet. There is no reason why this cannot occur if we want it to occur! We must begin with a far more thoughtful education. Our children must be raised differently. The movies, theater, television, and music must all radically change as a new consciousness pervades God's Earth. Yes, it is God's Earth as all of us are God's Children badly misbehaving.

There must be a mass commitment to spiritual growth as each individual follows his or her subjective pathway. Each of us is on a different spiritual rung, so there is no one path appropriate for all. That is an essential understanding. The knowledge that we are all Children of God can be established on Earth whenever we care enough to do so. Fear cannot prevent it from happening. Caring and love can bring it to pass. Our leaders will make it happen when they realize that there is no other way to achieve harmony and peace. A life of war, poverty, and attacks on nature are our current status, and these features of Earth life must become completely unacceptable to civilized people. These objectives will not come about until there is a new consciousness that everyone and everything is God's and that we are all God's Children. Life is to be encountered as such. There is no alternative!

The dedication to bring in a new expanded consciousness must grip humankind as we finally recognize that mutual destruction will lead nowhere but to mutual destruction. Who wants to be the last one standing? And for what? Who wants civilization to be lost to violence? A general growth in consciousness will be firmly established only when there is the understanding that the current road ahead is suicide for all humanity!

If we *must* fight another, let us realize that we have both lost even before the fight has begun. With that understanding we may decide that there is a better way to resolve apparent differences. Using violence to resolve disputes is not the way of a God-loving people. The permanent connection to God is at the core of each of us, and we should live in justice and peace. To harm or neglect another does violence to that connection to the eternal One. There is no reason to remain where we are. A New Consciousness will dawn if and when it is wanted badly enough. It certainly is needed now.

Silence Is Golden

"Silence Is Golden" is quite an expression. It allows us to listen to each other rather than just to express our own opinions. We all can learn much by really listening to each other, but the greatest act of silence is the act of meditation. When we pray we speak to the spiritual world. When we meditate we can actually listen to the spiritual world and learn a great deal. If we are willing to relax and be in inner harmony, we meditate and connect to the spiritual world, to the Akashic Field. Meditation is the means we use to open gates of knowledge far ahead of contemporary thought. It is a means of traversing cultures and time if we are open to receive without bias. Meditation is, perhaps, one of the most important spiritual tools that we possess but there is a caution. Meditation is so powerful that it must be kept in balance. In our book, *Universal Kabbalah: Dawn of a New Consciousness,* we suggested four basics to your daily activity. They are:

- Studying
- Praying
- Meditating and chanting
- Doing good deeds and service to others

By the age of seventeen, it is to be hoped that one has been through a process of natural development of body and mind, including wide reading in the wisdom literature of several spiritual traditions, as well as attainment of a certain groundedness in the physical and emotional realms. Meditation now can be a needed vehicle for further growth and integration with the spiritual world. Meditation can bring into one's life a maturity that will allow recognition of inner attachments and habits of mind in regard to gender, nationality, class, religion, and even the negative ego—attachments of selfishness and greed. With practice in meditation, there comes a willingness to listen to the spiritual world as a Child of God *without* any of these attachments. If one can listen to the spiritual world naked, free of all those bindings, whatever is received

will be understood in a deeper part of the existential self. Let commitment to truth be your guide. Be open and serious about learning and
viewing the world through a most inclusive and mature lens.

I find that guided visualizations can be used in a neutral way when
they are divorced from all religious or gender implications. State clearly
at the beginning of your meditation that you are a Child of the Universe
who wishes a dialogue with the spiritual world, and that you wish to be
free of all preconceptions and are in a search for truth. Mean what you
say!

- Get yourself in a comfortable position. Sitting in a chair is fine.
- Feet are on the ground, back erect.
- Take four or five deep breaths. Be aware of them.
- Be in inner and outer harmony.
- Be open and without attachments.
- Move slowly (in your mind) into an area that you have planned to
  visit. This journey should take several minutes until you have lost
  awareness of the outside world and have completely focused on your
  journey. Focusing is the function of your Guided Visualization. When
  you have reached a clearly visualized destination, look around to see
  what entity may have come to meet you, then explain to that entity
  what you have come for. Listen in devotion. Remember, you have
  come to receive answers to your questions. Often the answers you
  receive are to be shared with other people in your life.
- Don't expect to be able to focus the first times that you "sit." This is a
  new activity and may take some time to master.
- When your meditation is completed, even if unsuccessful, go back
  slowly to your starting point, and from there reconnect with your
  physical environment. Don't be discouraged. This whole process of
  listening in devotion and silence may be very new to you. It is for
  most. It takes time to silence your thoughts. Listening to the spiritual
  world is one of the important parts of your life, often ignored in our
  time.

- This question arises: How do you know that what you are receiving is authentic? Listen to what you are being told carefully. There will be a very different quality to what is happening. It will be very different from anything else you ever experienced. It will also be positive. If authentic, it will be kind and helpful. It will bring you closer to others as a way of bringing you closer to the spiritual world. It will fill you with awe no matter how often you have succeeded in communicating. A new, vital step in your spiritual maturity has begun! You will become more loving, more creative, and you will go beyond the limitations of your self-centered ego. You will begin to understand Cosmic Consciousness! You will realize yourself as a Child of the Universe!

LEVEL 3. THE GRANDEUR OF A LOVE-FILLED MARRIAGE

If you have ever wondered about the importance of marriage, this account should answer your questions, even those that you never thought of asking. Lorraine has the following to contribute:

> *"For see, there nothing is in all the world*
> *But only love worth any strife or song or tear.*
> *Ask me not then to sing or fashion songs*
> *Other than this, my song of love to thee."*
> —FROM THE ARABIC, "THE CAMEL RIDER"

As a brief aside, we share the following: When the copyeditor set us searching for a source for this poem fragment, we were at first dismayed and then amazed at what we [Sheldon and Barbara] uncovered. Sheldon said, "Where to look? I have never heard of this poem, nor of any reference to it. This just came from Lorraine, and I wrote it down." After I [Barbara] spent a couple of hours looking for the proverbial needle

in that haystack we call the World Wide Web of information now stored
in cyberspace, I did find the poem from which the lines are taken. I
found *By Thy Light I Live: The Poetry of Wilfrid Blunt,* selected and arranged by
W.E. Henley and George Wyndham. It was published in London by
William Heinemann in 1898, and printed by Ballantyne, Hanson &
Co. of London and Edinburgh. The lines are found on page 273, taken
from the last stanza of "The Camel Rider." Looking further, I discovered that Wilfrid S. Blunt was born in 1840 and died in 1922. All this
certainly leaves me with some deep thoughts about the memory bank in
the Akashic Field.

It is not only remarkable that Sheldon was able to record this from
Lorraine's transmission, but also that I was able to locate the source.
This book is digitized by Google from its resting place in the Library
of the University of Michigan. I found the Google commentary rather
lovely and poetic in itself, and worthy of reproduction here:

This is a digital copy of a book that was preserved for generations on
library shelves before it was carefully scanned by Google as part of a
project to make the world's books discoverable online.

It has survived long enough for the copyright to expire and the book
to enter the public domain. A public domain book is one that was
never subject to copyright or whose legal copyright term has expired.
Whether a book is in the public domain may vary from country to
country. Public domain books are our gateways to the past, representing a wealth of history, culture, and knowledge that's often difficult
to discover.

Marks, notations, and other marginalia present in the original
volume will appear in this file—a reminder of this book's long journey from the publisher to a library and finally to you. Google's mission is to organize the world's information and to make it universally
accessible and useful.

To return to Lorraine's direct words:

Marriage is the single most important spiritual activity that you can engage in while on Earth. In your relationship to your spouse you intensify your relationship to the eternal One. You can even evaluate your love of the eternal One by your love of spouse. The most endearing pathway to the eternal One is through your love of God's creations. It is impossible to love the eternal One and not love God's creations. It is the true test of your spiritual state while on Earth. A love-bound marriage even gives you a partial insight into how relationships are conducted on this side. When love-bound spouses touch each other and embrace, they are actually nourishing each other by their loving energies.

Soul-mates are forever. More are needed. The love of each constantly nourishes the other. It flows with varying intensities depending on circumstances between them. When merging there is the greatest binding. Love always comes directly from the eternal One.

Only once was I able to see the love-glow radiating from your body. It came from the eternal One through me into you. You were completely filled with a golden glow.

For this reason all spiritual and religious leaders ought to be married in loving equality in order to fully understand the importance of a loving, sanctified relationship. Marriage on Earth can be a partial experience of heavenly relationships.

In America today, with a forty-nine percent divorce rate, we witness a complete misunderstanding of what marriage and all relationships are about. Marriage is a *sanctified* coming together of two souls. There is absolutely no thought of adultery in such a relationship. In fact, adultery prevents a deep love between spouses and destroys the nature of a love-bound marriage. Marriage is a spiritual love, not to be taken lightly. It is the essence of harmony. Our current state of marriage is so poor that many soul-mates are being asked to return to Earth at this time to be living demonstrations of a love-bound marriage. It is hoped that such living harmony will be an inspiration to so many others.

In our Earthly time we wanted to always be together. This was a liberating, helping experience. In order to do this as much as possible you moved from being a pre-law student at New York University to Long Island Ag and Tech so that we could share a farm and raise our children there with a model family cohesiveness. You then progressed to teacher of agriculture, a doctorate, and a university professorship. Early retirement allowed us to move to Ithaca, New York, where we could grow herbs in the summer and write in the winter. Our relationship was always close, joyful, and mutually nourishing. Even when we needed something from town we went together since togetherness was what our lives were all about.

In those rides, or those we took in the evening or on weekends, it was just the two of us, taking joy in being near each other. It was so good! We each helped the other grow, sharing spiritual insights and prayers, even meditations. Almost every evening we would sit together on the couch and continue our discussions and insights. With soft music playing in the background there was always time for swaying together. It was always wonderful closeness. We were one in every way, as it is supposed to be. Neither you nor I ever took a separate vacation or an evening out because being together was our greatest joy. Since *we were two who had become one* our individual souls were each free to expand in spiritual nature. There was always constant support, and hugging was a daily activity that I looked forward to. It happened several times a day. Most people don't realize that a loving marriage is so liberating, not stifling as many have found. They have no idea of what a loving marriage could bring. They never tried to bring theirs to fruition.

Marriage is a sacred meeting where each tries to help the other on their mutual journey. Such a journey could not be accomplished alone since you need the unity of male and female to provide balance, support, and love. Such a marriage would be the beginning of understanding the true goals for each individual and what unity can mean on Earth. If two could not become one they could never hope to understand how the human family could become one! They would miss their most important meeting and an opportunity for learning on Earth. Each day is to be made holy and is to begin with the one closest to you, your spouse—only then can you move outward! You will then be able to arrive before the eternal One in peace, for the path is one of love. When you live in *love* there is no finite separation between you, your spouse, humanity, and the eternal One. You are living your soul life! *All is unity!*

LEVEL 2. LOVE, KNOWLEDGE, COMPASSION, TRUTH, AND RESPONSIBILITY

Love

When Lorraine was in the hospital near the end of her time on the Earth, she thought that she would come home to Ithaca and said that her next series of paintings would be about God's love. (Recall that the series she had just completed was her mystical interpretation of the Hebrew alphabet, a series filled with beauty and awesome energy.) Sharing her knowledge of God's love is a subject very close to her heart. She now volunteered the following:

The love of the eternal One is the cement that holds the universe together. That kind of love is incomprehensible to humankind. It is beyond human capacity to even begin to understand the force of that love. Just a small part of that love is what sustains the world, and an even smaller part of that love is the source of human love and creativity. Without love and passion we could do little of lasting value on Earth or on This Side. They are our foundation, our rock—the launch pad for our efforts. Love and passion accompany us on our journey and make it all possible. They are the twin blessings for the long road ahead.

Without the twin blessings of love and passion our insight would be almost non-existent, our outcomes mediocre. Love and passion take us toward the light with beauty and wonder as our companions.

Whenever there is love between one and another, God's presence is also there. Our love is a very, very small part of the love of the eternal One. This love is available for those open to it regardless of religious affiliation, nationality, or gender. It is only humans who have self-centered egos, who are narrow and bigoted and have little or no understanding of the power of God's love.

Those who harbor hatred have never been aware of God's love, for having known this love there is no room for hatred. Those who would seek out another to instigate violence have never known God's love. To be fully open to God's love is to recognize the spark of God in all individuals. It is not necessary to like another to love them. Love the spark, dislike the evil deeds!

Spiritual love is forever; it follows to This Side. Physical love quickly loses its force after we have crossed over. There is nothing of greater beauty than the spiritual love which creates the universe and of which we may partake. My thought paintings here are my feeble attempt to picture "God's Love" in recognizable form. God's love is awesome. To be bathed in it is sublime.

Every profound sexual experience is a loving act. The biblical word for sexual intercourse is *YADA*. It literally means "loving embrace." It also has the meaning of "knowing." To know someone or something is to embrace the object or the person with love. *At the core of all significant relationships is a heart filled with love!*

Loving another person is a step on the road to loving God. Loving all of creation is a step on the road to loving God. It is in loving God's creations that we love God. All that is is holy. We can awaken to that reality. We can make it so in our eyes. That is a large part of our mission.

Knowledge

Many people on Earth, especially those in modern America, don't
understand what the concept of cognition or knowledge is all about.
They think that it only pertains to the intellect, but psychologists and
philosophers know better. They know, as Kabbalah pointed out so long
ago, that a complete knowledge—called *da'at*—is an equal blending of
intellect and loving intuition. Only the two together give you the perfection of knowledge. It also signifies that only in having the two in
equal balance, male and female, would we have the conditions for a
viable civilization. The eternal One doesn't discriminate between the
genders or favor one gender over another. Why should we? More
people on Earth are slowly awakening to that realization.

To educate children with only intellect as a foundation for life is
also to give them a perception of pure materialism. It is an education
for out-of-balance analytical individuals. It subverts their spiritual
understanding, which can only be reached with a loving intuition. With
this understanding you can see that our finest schools, even our "religious schools," are often teaching a distorted, materialistic view of
reality. This has been called a "spiritual materialism." Yes, there are
some schools blending intuition and intellect together but they are
very few. Remember these two elements must be blended together in
education. In educating children, it is not enough to simply have art or
music follow the intellectual lessons. Indeed these must be blended
together in our schools and in our lives. Such blending in harmony
leads to the experiencing of the eternal One, in pure love, not merely
intellectualism.

I am being very personal here since I want to provide some first-hand
examples. I have visited schools, both public and independent, for many
years. I visited one Catholic school where the principal, a physically
small Sister but mentally a giant, stated that hers was a "Martin Buber
school." Her teachers, from a midwestern order, truly understood the

philosophy and tried to introduce music and art into the curricula. They blended their presentations. The children loved their Sisters and often went to the convent after school. The good Sisters even tried to reduce class size from fifty to twenty-five. The priest of the parish called the Sisters lazy and had them all removed. His reasoning prevailed. Many other church schools in the New York City area were under similar direction.

I spoke with the head of the Jewish Board of Education in New York City, and I explained that the state of Hebrew School education was deplorable. It completely lacked balance. She simply could not understand. The students had their intellectual studies in the morning and had music the last period of the day. She couldn't believe that balance could or should be brought to all lessons. She should have known better!

I spoke to the Supervisor of Education of the Rockville Center Diocese, who was aware of the one-sided view of life reinforced by computer-based education. He also believed that it would prove harmful to human relations, and our view of the world, over an extended period of time. To his regret, parental pressure forced him to go along with the introduction of computers at an early age.

It is important to understand that what I write of is being done right now. There is an older school system that understands the "knowledge" composite and is properly utilizing it. I refer to the Waldorf Schools. They understand the twin components of knowledge and try to keep that balance in their teaching. They teach through beauty and wonder, from pre-kindergarten to the completion of high school, and have their graduates accepted in the finest colleges and universities in the country. They can bring much to society. It is being done so we know that it can be done if we want it done! Do we care enough to have it done? That is always the real question. I am sure that there are other schools offering a fine education. I am writing about only that which I have experienced.

If you want to pursue the question of how to educate children, seek out Jack Petrash, a former Waldorf teacher, or Dr. Jeff Kane, Vice-President of Long Island University. Their knowledge of the subject will meet and exceed all your expectations.

Compassion

When you have succeeded in removing the fences that separate you from another, you will be able to feel the pain of that other, sometimes very acutely, if you both are in a very loving relationship. Let me provide one example. When Lorraine gave birth to Jesse, our first son, she experienced a very painful seventeen-hour labor. When she finally gave birth, at 2 a.m., I left the hospital and drove home. I was experiencing severe discomfort in my abdominal area. When I undressed the reason was apparent. My entire abdominal area was bright red from a very severe rash. In a state of compassion, I had felt her pain in that entire area. It couldn't have been more obvious.

A compassionate relationship is one of deep caring in an endeavor to remove suffering. Compassion for others is vital on the spiritual journey. Not only are you then a caring individual, you have a commitment of responsibility for all others, human and animal alike, however close or distant. Compassionate responsibility is a worldview with *no distinctions.* All others are perceived as Children of God and you, as a Child of God, have a kinship relationship to all people and all creatures and all of nature at all times.

Lorraine adds:

Our acts of compassion are basic to all civilized relationships and are an absolute necessity on the ladder of spiritual growth. Life on Earth could not function in any stable, positive, mature fashion without continuous acts of compassion. Such acts are as essential to civilization as food and water. Current wars, poverty, and general violence to people and nature alike are a firm indication of the need to begin to act with a far greater degree of compassion. So far, humans have failed the test.

By relating compassionately to all our fellow people and creatures, all Children of God, we are also relating to their creator, our creator, the eternal One. *All loving, caring, compassionate, responsible relationships take us to the eternal One!* There are many rungs on the ladder of spiritual growth that must be climbed in order to reach our destination.

Truth

Some might question the inclusion of the concept of "truth" as a subject to be studied on the Other Side, especially at such a high level of importance. In seeking to encounter the eternal One in meditations I have always been faced with a love of enormous magnitude, but reduced so that I could be in relationship with it. I've also always perceived a purity to it that was joined to the concept of "truth."

The eternal One creates us with "free will of thinking." We often misuse the gift, and it's our misuse that creates evil. We receive a magnificent gift of free choice and throughout history have often misused it. Our souls were created with the ability, honed by repeated incarnations, to grow to spiritual maturity. Fundamental to that growth is our creation in the image of the eternal One. That image is one of love and the purity and holiness of truth. If we really wish to climb the top rungs of the spiritual ladder, our lives must be based on that love, that purity and holiness of truth. The truth that we may perceive on Earth is not the whole truth of the Other Side. Our highest understanding of truth, a human truth, can only be arrived at by going forth naked, before God, while suspending for the duration of the meditation specific thought patterns associated with disparate religions.

By living a life in the purity and holiness of truth, you are living a life in the image of God. This suggestion is a simple one but so difficult for humans to fulfill.

Responsibility

In Lorraine's words again:

Each of us comes to Earth with a mission to perform. Some missions seem great. Some seem small. For each of us, male or female, the individual mission is ours to fulfill. To the individual the mission, of whatever size, is an individual responsibility. We chose it, for good reasons, before incarnation. It has become our responsibility and we are accountable to ourselves for fulfilling it at this intended hour of our existence. If we fail because we placed our soul in the shadows, we will hold ourselves accountable when we return to This Side. We will desperately want to heal the life we forfeited on Earth.

Viewing our faults during our Life Review will, in itself, be a painful and discouraging process. Our souls want to be accountable, and we will view our failures with dismay. We will have endless time to live with our lack of responsibility on Earth, and there will be guidance and solitude to help us reflect and mature.

When ready, we will follow the trail back to Earth for healings whenever possible. In our souls *we are responsible for all our acts, and we will allow nothing to deter us from our healing and the healing of those whom we may have violated. Our souls would do no less.*

I rejoice in the knowledge that I, only I, am responsible for the entirety of my life. I plan it in peace and harmony on This Side, though I may be weak when the opportunities for growth on Earth present themselves. If so, I truly let myself down and those who believe in me. After many lessons and experiences I *will* grow and I *will* be responsible for every step I take on this very long spiritual path.

Since we are all attached to the eternal One at the upper soul level, we are all related. It is to the eternal One that we have our ultimate attachment and responsibility.

There is never an escape from responsibility because our soul always welcomes it and actually wants responsibility for its actions every minute of every day of every year throughout timeless eternity! Only a life of responsibility is a life of significance. A life without responsibility is a life of chaos.

My entire life is holy, as is yours. If I falter I will reclaim my responsibilities and heal as I go forward!

LEVEL 1. ONENESS *(THE GOAL)*

Other designations for this level might be: God, Allah, Krishna, The Eternal One, The Almighty, The Great Spirit, and so on.

Lorraine's contribution began during my morning meditation:

I had been asked to enter Level One training some time ago. There were two reasons. First, I was ready. Second, I needed the experience and knowledge so that I could transmit it to you for the book. The experience was the culmination of my life. When you cross over I will gladly accompany you through it. It is a golden point of existence! In our next incarnation on Earth we will be able to better represent the Oneness because of the experience here. You will be filled with a love and knowledge beyond present human comprehension. We need both—the experiences learned on Earth and the knowledge and experiences gained here. Either side alone is incomplete.

Once, before time began, there was only God, the Oneness. For reasons that we cannot fully know, God, out of itself, created the beginning, and the universe came into being. Yes, the Oneness is the creator of the suns, the stars, the galaxies, worlds without end and also all peoples and all of nature. All of this is being created and sustained by the Oneness.

The universe was born in love and is sustained in love.
The universe was born in love and is sustained in love.

So time began. Everything and everyone came from the Oneness, and it all is sustained by the love of the Oneness. The Oneness brought forth all that there is and for that my love and gratitude are unbounded. The highest praise for God is to live in God's image— that of loving without end.

We, and that means every single one of us, and everything that there is in the universe, came from the Oneness. We are all part of the Oneness, for there is at the core of each of us the spark of the Oneness that we call our soul. It is always connected to God. We may call it our soul or our consciousness, but it was given to each of us in love by the Oneness. It alone is our salvation and our eternal life.

When you are in the middle of a pool of water there is no need to reach out for water. We are all in the middle of the pool of love, only on this Side we know where we are. Our goal, always, is to take away the blinders for all on Earth so that they will know who they are and where they are.

We are all within God. We are living within the Oneness. We are all Children of God. What better charge upon us than to always be aware of the Oneness and to help, with our love and caring, all other Children of God?

Killing, hatred, anger, greed, and miserable behavior are a crime against God, our creator. So few on Earth realize this. Their selfish- ness has replaced their creator as the source of their thinking and actions. Their choice is to be blind to their creator and their cre- ator's love. Their focus is on misery and pain. Their choice is to be blind to the sun, and they are nourished by a devouring self-cen- teredness.

Some have walked away from the Oneness and have chosen immediate gratification for a brief second of their existence. With profound regret will they enter their Life Review. With horror will *they experience their Review and fully realize the failure of their incarnation, one in which their accomplishments could have brought Light to people everywhere. They will do much to correct their past behaviors. They will have guides to advise their actions.*

Selfish action accounts for world destructiveness and misery. Action from your essence, the spark of the Oneness, is always able to be known. We are all within the Oneness, so choose wisely no matter where you are.

There are none outside the Oneness. There is no place else to go. There is no space outside the Oneness. There is no place any of us would wish to go. Only by hallowing the all do we approach the One. The all lives in the Oneness.

It, our soul, is to evolve through many incarnations into a completely spiritual entity as a helper devoted to God. At some distant point of time after the Oneness began the creation of the physical universe, the physical universe will no longer be needed.

What will remain will be the individual sparks, now helpers, who will have climbed the ladder of spirituality in order to be near God. All were created in love and responsibility. All may choose to climb the ladder. It is always our free choice. We are always related in the Oneness, and we are always related to the each and the all.

The each and the all are bound together by bonds of love, often placed in the shadows. We all can live in freedom. It is only love that eternally brings us together. Each moment we may also choose separation. We are always free to choose! Free choice and responsibility for our actions are always basic to life.

The Oneness continues to choose our creation in love. We are always given our free will. There is nothing outside the Oneness.

The universe was born in love and is sustained in love.
The universe was born in love and is sustained in love.

I am in God and the spark of God is in me and in everyone and everything that exists or ever will exist. To always act in love is my greatest wish.

The Oneness is beyond our world, beyond our world God. Out of the Oneness creation began in love. All is sustained in love so we call the Oneness SHE. SHE is loving and nurturing, though no gender is implied. She is the universe! All is holy.

Our understanding of the world, both physical and spiritual, is a process of the evolution of ideas on the physical plane as well as the involution of concepts from the spiritual domain. There is no downside to living a noble and productive life. There is no downside to living a life as a child of God with the knowledge that we are all children of God, the eternal One.

CHAPTER 8

Soul Life on the Other Side

"As Above,
So Below.
As Below
So Above."

"Thou shalt love Thy Neighbor as Thyself."
—DEUTERONOMY 18:18

The basic fact of life on the Other Side is that our relationships with all others are part of our relationship to the eternal One. There is no separation between them. That truth also applies to life on Earth. Most of us haven't arrived at that realization yet. Our relationship to all "things" is precisely the same. All is holy. That means that it is not only people who are holy but that all of nature is holy. Every person, every animal, every bit of nature is a gift of God. Each and every relationship should be approached in an I—Thou manner. Forget your self-consciousness. Live from your heart. Live in community with others. *Never* forget who you are and who all others are, *Children of God.* Your life here is a dance of gratitude, joy, and *love for the eternal One and all creations of the eternal One.* We know that we are always in God. We are all bound together in love bestowed by the eternal One who always surrounds us. Sadly, so few on Earth realize this truth of truths. It is the essential fact of creation. It is never forgotten on This Side. It is the core of the harmony that is lived here. We are brothers and sisters on the journey of existence. We are *responsible* for each other; there is no separation between us. We are also responsible to ourselves. If we have strayed and committed evil, we *will* correct what needs to be corrected. We will receive help as needed, not punishment. We will make amends. That is our urgent need, and we will satisfy it both here and when returning to Earth.

As Lorraine emphasizes, this general understanding is what draws souls together on the Other Side. There is the common knowledge of who each is and the knowledge that as Children of God we are responsible, grateful, and loving to God and loving to all of God's creations. The boundaries between us have diminished and faded away. There is no such thing or Being as an independent reality here or on Earth or any-where in creation! Lorraine's contribution seemed to start from the middle of a thought:

The painting series *On God's Love* is doing just fine. I create each one slowly in my mind and project it. It remains as long as I wish it to. They will be here to share with you. I've done six so far. Some are beautiful landscapes that I see here. Several are of a light-filled sky. One is of a newborn infant. One is of us together. They are all reflections of God's love made manifest.

When not in schooling, which we have discussed at length, or when I'm mind-painting, I spend much time speaking (though it is not speech as on the Earth) with Loretta and Natalie [friend and cousin]. We often try to help souls who have passed over from the war. We even attend concerts. Music compositions are often sent to Earth (through intuitive projections by others) to be shared. That is also true of writing and all art forms and other aspects of knowledge. Only advanced souls can do this, and it is always for the benefit of humankind. I find myself more and more interested in this direction. It is one that we need to do together. It is a step forward in our future. We will be transmitters if you agree.

Music is a very important part of our awakening here. It is also a vital part of holy married love in this community. It is most joyful. I'm so glad that we shared classical music on Earth. There are even structures here used for praying. All denominations can be found here, and they are used by the younger souls. Older souls attend a temple that focuses on the eternal One, with no particular attachment to any religion. It seems more honest that way since I and the others in our community have experienced most religions and see no need for a filtering device. We spend much time singing beautiful hymns and also chanting. You will like it and we can go often. It's a wonderful thing to do. It helps bring us closer to the eternal One. For a change, we sometimes visit various denominations when they have prayer meetings. The singing is lovely and all are welcome. Relationships are always honored and we always feel attached to each other. We always feel comfortable and caring toward each other. We also visit other communities when there are events of interest.

I have mind-created a duplicate of our land and house in Ithaca which I retreat to fairly often. It will be here for us when you join me. It is so peaceful and is a good place for me to rethink our past life together. When I go there I usually bring Jezebel or Macabee [two of the eight dogs that we shared at different times during our marriage] because we enjoy being together and I'm not completely alone then. I have even mind-created Treman Falls. It's a real Power Center, and meditating there helped me very much while I was on Earth. I recall walking with you, Ellen, and Larry (after I passed over) when the three of you visited the falls. You were aware of my presence and told them that I was with all of you. It did me so much good.

I do miss you even though part of your soul still remains. It's not the same without the rest of you. Loretta, Natalie, and I often have long talks together about our past life and how we can always improve. It's interesting how we remember all the details, so there is much to discuss. Being more open and sharing is high on our list of things that we can improve upon. Being genuinely interdependent has such a high priority here. It's an essential for spiritual growth. We are all Children of God but rarely act that way on Earth. Here, it is so different. Don't get me wrong. None of us are Divine but here, we are all honest and caring and our sense of humor has not been left behind. We are all very willing to look at our faults and learn from them. We see the whole picture, and most of us are anxious to move forward. It can and should be the same on Earth. Enough is known about spirituality if people want to know. Most people on Earth seem not to care to know. That's the real problem. Too many people avoid thinking! That seems to be the mark of all fundamentalists. Real thinking would require major changes in lifestyle. It would entail their being responsible, open, and willing to search for the truth. That's one of the purposes of returning to Earth. We can also learn to be noble in a physical form in spite of all of the seductions. Then it's real growth that will happen continuously.

Loretta's last-minute suppers in Greenport, always made on the spur of the moment, are a good example of a caring relationship. All good relationships are always high on our agendas. We know that we are all related, but on Earth very few of us act that way. Narrowness and fundamentalism have become a way of life for so many.

Regardless of what topic we choose to discuss, close relationships are always prominent. I am so happy that we have been so very close, at one, for so very, very long. We will continue to be so. It's not curtailing. It's liberating as we help each other grow, and we fill each other with joy. People on Earth sometimes wonder if there is sex here. There is in a way, but it's much different. Obviously there is no physical body to deal with. Here, we merge our energy forms and we can communicate in the deepest, most sensitive way. It's a very complicated issue.

I merged with you once when you were very lonely after I passed over. You had asked for some message that evening and I gave you what you needed. I sent waves of "peace" to you as I surrounded you with love. We both benefited greatly from that experience.

Here, such things are generally confined to soul-mates, which is as it should be. There is no "womanizing" or "adultery," as most souls do not take gender forms as soul-mates do.

Soul-mates are united forever and would not even think of straying. You and I are a very good, loving, productive unit.

One of our tasks on Earth was to be a model for successful marriage. Such tasks have also been asked of others because the need is so great on Earth. We were asked to go as the others have. Most people have forgotten that *marriage is a sacred relationship*. It is very special and should always be treated as a true gift, not to be made commonplace.

On Earth people in a sanctified love can begin to approximate merging as it is here. It is one of the greatest gifts that you can give to another. The individuals can hug and caress and be as intimate as possible without sexual involvement. It can become a time of being quiet and being at one with the other. It is a valuable time of non-verbal embrace. Such embrace would have a profound impact.

If I had to pick out one important feature here that is in short supply on Earth it would have to be the abundance of wonderful, joyous, loving relationships. That is the key to harmony. The closer we are to others, the greater becomes our love for the eternal One because we see and literally feel God's presence as our love and joy blossom. You literally feel God in all of your caring and loving relationships. There are always three present, not just two. Without the presence of the eternal One, there would be no binding together because the love comes initially from God. It is the glue of creation, the bliss of encounter.

Drawings of the Other Side

These illustrations were very difficult to complete. With considerable effort I received views of the Other Side that Lorraine said should be included in the book. I made rough drawings and sent them on to Joshua, my son, who has done many pen and ink drawings for his books. The beautiful finished products are his. That must have been quite a task for him to complete. My only advice to him was to pray and meditate before each drawing. A special note about the drawing of the Taj Mahal: Lorraine said that this entire structure was designed in heaven then constructed on Earth.

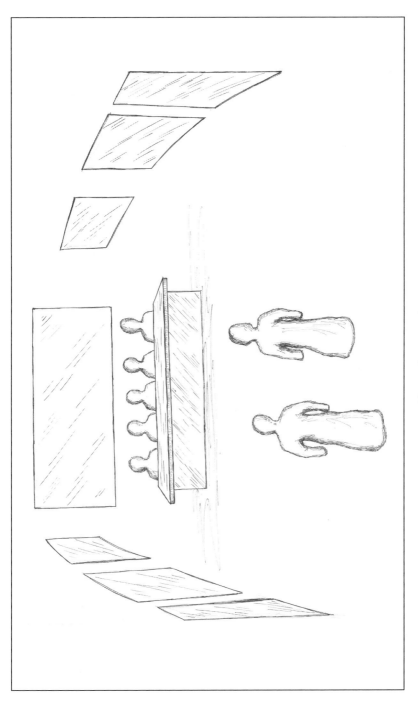

Life Review Session

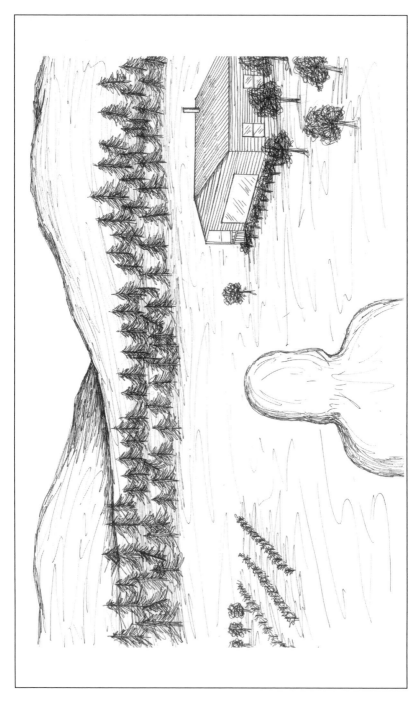

Temple Structure: Energy Forms Dancing

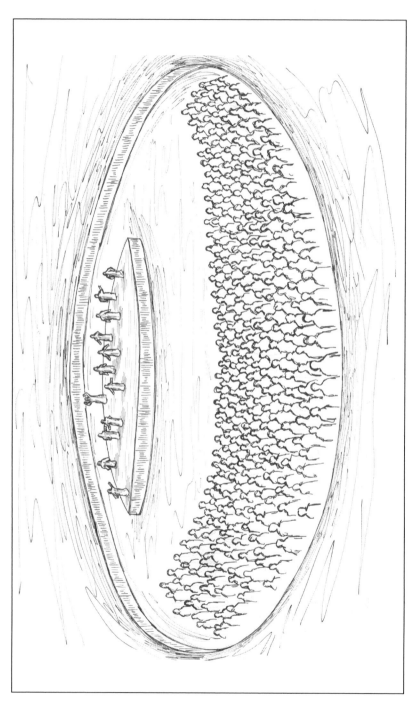

Recreation

Two Soul-Mates Merging, Surrounded by the Love of God

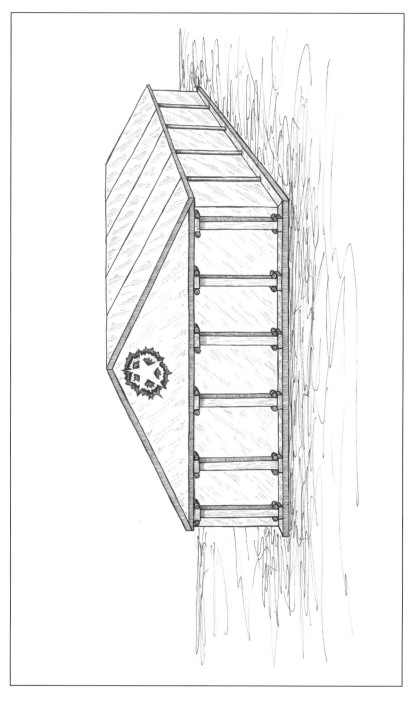

A Temple for Prayer

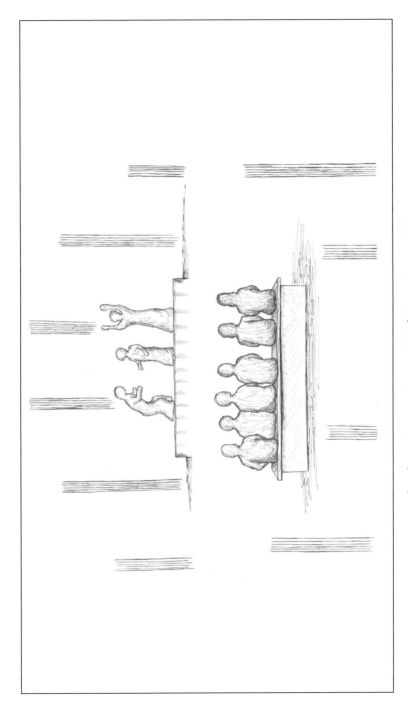

Schooling: Energy Forms Watching a Presentation
Many Energy Forms Seated, Watching Other Energy Forms on Stage

The Taj Mahal, where Marriage Ceremonies are Held for Soul-Mates.
(The building on Earth in Agra, India, was constructed from plans sent down from the Other Side.)

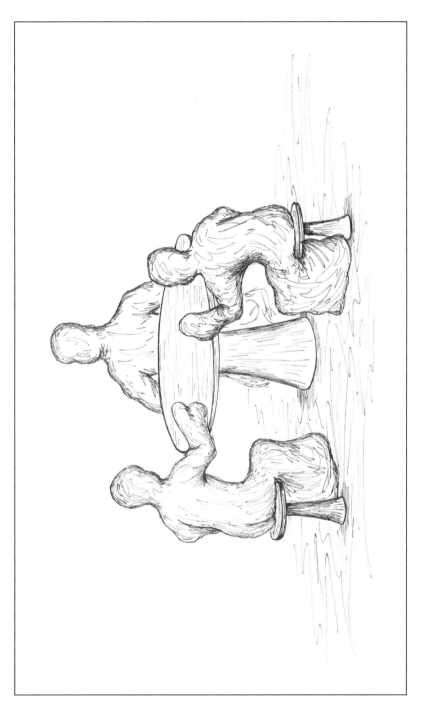

Counseling Prior to Transition to the Physical

CHAPTER 9

Counseling Prior to Transition to the Physical

From Lorraine:

I arranged our next incarnation. The country is fixed. It will not be in America. We'll discuss the time when you cross over. It's a good thing that we talked about this while we were together on Earth. That made it so much easier for me. Now let me contribute a description of a typical transition from here to the physical plane. Remember, before we attempted to conceive a child we prayed that we might have a child "who would walk with God." Knowing our disposition, it was easier for our two children to select us. Prayers prior to the attempt at conception are so important, as are prayers of gratitude after the birth. Pray that you will be able to provide your child what you were selected for, and also pray that you may learn the lessons your child has to teach.

When you're ready your guides assess that it is now time for another learning and healing time of physical experience on Earth. You have undertaken periods of solitude and reflection, and there have been extensive sessions with one or more guides who have helped make your last incarnation as meaningful as possible. They and you now believe that you are ready for Earth. They have discussed and prepared you with the knowledge of the lessons that both you and they feel you are ready for. You may even have had helping discussions with the Wise Ones. This next incarnation will also be one of healing and growth, as have been all the others. These experiences on Earth are necessary if there is to be lasting spiritual growth for you and for others, and although you don't look forward to leaving the beautiful environment of This Side, you know that Earthly visits are a necessity to test and improve your spiritual growth in action.

Some choices that you make allow for more rapid growth on Earth, as they are more difficult. Some choices are mainly for healing of self and others. You view these as absolutely necessary and you will select these as soon as you are prepared for them. Indeed, in some choices you place yourself in positions of leadership in order to assess if you can handle them with caring and responsibility. These often prove to be the most difficult since there are so many temptations along the way. The failure rate is often high, and guides have much to undo when you return. You may return haunted by your failures and thus be in great need of help in your recovery. We all realize that time on Earth presents opportunities, and perhaps pain and suffering. It is both a harsh and beautiful school where we can grow through testing and *overcoming temptation*. Each incarnation is the culmination of our lessons and also of loving preparation by your guides here. Each incarnation may also be viewed as an examination on Earth that must be passed in order to prove that you have mastered your lessons and now have the ability to move up the spiritual ladder.

An incarnation is so important that a soul never does choose it in isolation. There are guides and even Wise Ones who may be called on for insight and discussion. A great deal of preparation must be accomplished by your guides so that plans on Earth will mesh. That takes considerable effort prior to your incarnation. Think of all the planning that must be done so that the timing of events will be synchronized. Even your computers on Earth would find that a formidable task. We all have such good thoughts here but they may quickly fade before powerful Earthly temptations. Realize that the temptations seem to be growing on Earth, fed by our failures in a past or current life. In preparation for this latest incarnation we have reviewed many of our past lives and concentrated on our errors. We know how difficult it is to remain true to our objectives, but we will go confident of our abilities because of the help that we have received and the care that we have taken. We now have the courage to heal past misdeeds and trust that we will not weaken as we enter the trials of the Earth. Our sword will be that of caring, love, and responsibility for our actions. Our climbing actions have been defined and they will be our hidden motivation. This inner drive may become an open drive if we work hard enough to become aware of it. Always remember that in fulfilling your mission you are to be healing and loving. You are not returning to the Earth for a joyride!

Our guides have offered you several choices of parents who will provide the basis for accomplishing your goals. Your selection must also be based on proper time, religion, nationality, sex, body, and so on. Whether you remain with your first choices or leave them later in life, know the first choice was always taken for good reasons and was always the best available. The final birth selection is yours alone, even if you make a less-than-optimum choice. At this last moment your priorities may have changed for the worse. As we view life on Earth, and there are always such views available, there is always some fear and some trepidation. We want to improve our status but we are well aware of the difficulties and seductions awaiting us. If you know that you will have a partner with you on Earth it will ease the concern, but then you worry whether your meeting with the other will be accomplished. It is so important to keep to your unique task regardless of the temptations.

If we have been following the plan that we have devised for ourselves, with the help of others, we usually feel self-directed. Our life is progressing in an orderly, positive way. If we stray from our path we often feel that there is too much uncertainty in our life. It appears too disorganized. We seem to always be asking ourselves, "Why?" Meditation may often help a lost soul understand the situation and return to a projected mission. It all depends on our maturity and selflessness. It also depends on the nature of our mission and the dangers inherent in it. Sometimes the path that is our mission can be filled with pain, sometimes healing, sometimes love. We all have many incarnations because spiritual claim and responsibility are a giant leap. Do not think that a single incarnation is always all that is needed for a healing or to fulfill a spiritual task. Several incarnations may be needed in order to fully prepare you for an important mission.

We usually enter our mother's body a few months prior to birth. Time within the womb is boring and we often wander in and out. We are then not part of our chosen body but we are aware of the mother's emotions. We may, sometimes, even influence her actions. Some souls even join the baby shortly after birth. The time of joining is left to the incoming soul. If the birth is unsuccessful for any reason, we simply try again, often with the same parents. Souls are never, ever, lost this way. Sometimes the body passes over shortly after birth. The soul knew this prior to joining but needed a birth experience, so little was lost to the soul even with the birth pain involved. If all goes well and the birth is successful, the soul is usually delighted that the mission on Earth has begun. The soul's spiritual growth is so complicated that it is never wise to attempt to judge it. Our reasons for coming are always positive, even if we choose our own suffering, but we never, ever choose pain for others. That is a firm law! We would never think, on This Side, of harming another. We know that we are all related! We are still brothers and sisters while on Earth and we must communicate that to our chosen body. It is not an easy task when faced with so many Earthly temptations.

Even from this brief review you can see that full responsibility for all of our actions takes place here as well as on Earth. Over here we view this responsibility with joy. It is a key element in our freedom. I remember from my last time on Earth that there are many who would surrender their freedom to another. They have no understanding of how to mature spiritually or how to appreciate their free choices and a life of self-directed love. In time they will learn. Reincarnations allow the process of slow growth to happen. We cannot spiritually mature in only one attempt. Many reincarnations make the miracle possible. The process is absolutely wonderful!

CHAPTER 10

Soul-Mates and the Process of Creation

The *Zohar,* an important book of Kabbalah, states that "It is marriage that constitutes a difficult task for the Almighty because soulmates—male and female—are two halves of a single soul, split upon creation and sent their separate ways until, through successive incarnations, they have found correction sufficient to merit coming together again on this earth plane." Author Philip S. Berg (*Wheels of a Soul,* 1984, pp. 96–97) thus quotes the *Zohar* and goes on to write: "When soulmates meet and marry, knowingly or otherwise, they have agreed to co-star again with one they have known before in one or more lifetimes. The players, at any time, can alter the promise of the plot."

"What, then, is the God that is written about in the Bible? Kabbalists teach that the first line of Genesis has been badly mistranslated. Most people think it says: "In the beginning, God created the heavens and the earth." But the actual words in Hebrew can be read another way. A Kabbalist could say: 'With a beginning, (It) created God (Elohim, plural), the heavens and the earth.' That is to say, out of Nothingness the potential to begin was created—Beginningness. Once there was a beginning God (in a plural form) was created—a God to which the rest of us could relate. Then the heavens and the earth were created."
—DAVID COOPER, *GOD IS A VERB*

Lorraine, from Other Side, has now provided information to expand our picture of the spiritual world. The following paragraphs are based upon those transmissions:

Our understanding of the world, both physical and spiritual, is a process of the evolution of ideas on the physical plane as well as the involution of concepts from the spiritual domain. In that context let us explore the role of soul-mates in the unfolding of spiritual and physical worlds. We do know that love is the essential force that follows us on Both Sides, since it is a soul force. It is beyond physical love. Love is the prime force of the universe. Thus, loving relationships with nature, persons, and the spiritual are the core of our Being. This cannot and must not be denied! Love is our soul in essence. Love is our source for nobility. Love is always the guiding force in our lives, on both sides of the divide. Love is the binding force for soul-mates and is forever! Soul-mates are spiritually maturing Beings. Without identifying with the love force we all are shallow and distorted Beings adrift without our rudder. We are still in an adolescent stage of development.

Soul-mates rarely incarnate together. They often need different learning experiences on Earth. Since we usually do not perceive our "significant other" to be our soul-mate, the wisest and best course of action is to always treat others as Children of God deserving our best in love, action, and responsibility. Marriage is always a spiritual journey. Always treat it "as if" it were a constant test as well as an important force in our spiritual maturity. It should be unrivaled in our attention. That principle applies to all relationships that we attend to. Since we should be maturing at all times, this attitude could raise the level of all discourse to conscious participation in spiritual evolution. All marriages can be conceived of as being in one of four general categories:

• That based on physical attraction.
• Plus that based on emotional attraction
• Plus that based on knowledge, awareness, and consciousness attraction
• Plus that based on a spiritual binding = soul-mates.

Now, it is time to explain the vital importance of soul-mates on Earth and on This Side. When soul-mates are together on Earth it is usually because two are required in order to achieve a needed emphasis or direction. The most obvious example has been the need for the presence of volunteer soul-mates to serve as models for happy, unified marriages, a true partnership relationship of equals. Since America has a divorce rate of approximately fifty percent, and happy, productive marriages form the basis for the flowering of communities, here and throughout the Earth, it was deemed necessary to send many soul-mates to America and other countries in order to renew the force for substantial marriages. This change for the positive will be seen as current difficulties are overcome. Soul-mates who have united even though incarnating separately also have achieved a degree of spiritual maturity that enables them to make decisions and live a noble life. There is no downside to living a noble and appropriately productive life.

When on This Side, soul-mates help others and each other to keep on with the process of spiritual growth and responsibility. They often share tasks and are always helpers in their communities. They join the ranks of a stable, loving, productive contingent.

There is an ancient symbol, found in the antiquity of India and in the goddess religions and later in Judaism, which expresses in one image much of what we endeavor to communicate here. So rich and complex is this ancient symbol, a thorough discussion of its associations within our collective consciousness would require volumes, but for our purposes here we point toward the concept of union, the *Six-Pointed Star,* where the triangles together symbolize perfection in the blending of intuition and intellect. This blending in the active function of intuition and intellect is a sublime achievement as the individual soul strives toward authentic Being and the actualization of the union of heaven and Earth.

As played out on Earth, the Six-Pointed Star also stands for the Sacred Union, the chalice and the blade, the equal and balanced union of the masculine and the feminine energies, male and female, the most powerful meditation symbol we are aware of. The masculine-feminine energies intertwined become the *Sacred Union.* This symbol speaks volumes without uttering a single word. We have only to listen in silent meditation in order to restore it for our own sake, and certainly for the benefit of the world.

King David selected this ancient symbol of the Sacred Union, the balance of the masculine and the feminine energies, as the emblem on his shield in order to speak to his soldiers of the fight more noble. And so must we, as individuals, evolve toward a full-spectrum integration—through a dynamic and creative interaction centered in the heart—of these fundamental polarities here on Earth.

With this as important background, let us continue with an example of tasks to be accomplished. Lorraine, after she crossed over in April 2001, helped bring over soldiers who had passed during war. She tells me that both she and I will serve as "transmitters" when we complete our incarnations on the Earth. It will be our chosen task to furnish some individuals on Earth with artistic and theological concepts, just as these have been forwarded to us when we were on Earth. While on Earth, concepts are continually sent to those open to receive them and have served as the basis for much of our growth in all areas of life—ranging from architecture to literature to theology to music, and so on.

After performing selective tasks on This Side, soul-mates can be admitted to the highest and most respected task. They can serve as "Wise Ones" or "Elders" in Life Reviews and can also advise as needed. Wise

Ones are always soul-mates though they may not always serve together on the same Life Review.

After continued growth in spiritual maturity and responsibility, soul-mates, now Wise Ones, can be requested by the Oneness to perform as Gods in helping co-create other worlds, of which there are uncounted numbers in the universe. (The current estimate is that there are at least ten billion Earth-like planets in our beautiful universe.) There is much to do. Our new task in an emerging world is our pinnacle of growth and responsibility. There is always the Oneness who created all that is. In our new responsibility we are always near the Oneness. Looked at in another way, it is easy to see that in our repeated times on Earth we are really *Gods in Training*. With this awareness each life takes on new meanings of responsibility and love. How can you live in boredom or hatred or even see reason in war when once you realize who you are and what your goal is? Can there be a greater responsibility than to be a God in Training?

The God of each new world is always composed of two soul-mates, together One. The One God is always composed of soul-mates continuing their productive, loving life together. The act of creation requires two. The female component is often called the Goddess, Divine Mother, Sophia, and so on. In Hebrew she is called the Shechinah, the indwelling female presence. The male component is often called in Hebrew Adonai. There are many other names for both. The Goddess is always our constant companion. A life of prayers to the Goddess will aid in the growth of your spiritual maturity. The Goddess is a soul-mate who has achieved her full potential. The male God is background, the maintainer. He is a soul-mate who has achieved his full potential. Together they are One, One God. Two forming One. That is an eternal truth.

Above the level of a world God is the Oneness, not even known to us in meditation. Each of us is, in truth, an energy in the process of becoming. Looked at through this lens, we can see why our road is so long and, at times, so difficult. We have much to experience, and much to learn.

> This is a crucial time in the history of this world. It is of vital importance that the feminine energy enter again more fully into our consciousness and stand beside the masculine energy—Shechinah and Adonai standing together on the open sunrise shell.
>   There is the One God;
>   The Oneness is God.

Postscript

I have been on a remarkable journey! After writing two books (*Universal Kabbalah: Dawn of a New Consciousness* and *The Western Book of Crossing Over: Conversations with the Other Side*, both completed with much help) about the spirituality of life and existence on both sides of the diminishing divide, I would like to conclude with some "realizations" that I have been thinking about morning, noon, and night. Some of them lead me to make suggestions that would require a vast change in the orientation of our mind-set. The changes will also bring a bit of the Other Side to our doorstep. We have it in our power to bring peace and harmony to this wonderful planet of ours, or we will simply destroy much of life. What we need is the courage to act in caring, responsibility, and love.

- The information in this book would be unnecessary if sufficient numbers of people on Earth truly followed a spiritual pathway of love and brotherhood. The wars, the poverty, the bigotry, and the greed show that this is not now so. Hence, to partially answer our needs, such help is provided by the Other Side here as necessary.
- These two books (*Universal Kabbalah: The Dawn of a New Consciousness* and *The Western Book of Crossing Over: Conversations with the Other Side*) were written to "help people." This can be done only if each of us individually is willing to grow spiritually, to intentionally work to expand our consciousness, and thus finally to know ourselves as responsible "Children of the Universe" with a sacred spark within.
- For each of us to communicate with spiritual reality without bias, to any extent possible, we have to go beyond *all*

preconceived notions and approach the spiritual, and each
other, unencumbered by patterns in the socially and religiously
mediated personal unconscious. This is not to devalue
acculturation and religion, but to put meditation in perspective
as a vehicle with the possibility to take us to the spiritual gateway.
From that point we approach only in pure love. To condition
our expectations according to religious affiliation when
meditating can limit and distort what we may receive.

· It is always important to remember that in our various
incarnations we have had many diverse cultural and religious
experiences that have shaped our growth. The golden thread that
connected them all is that we were always, are always, and will
always be Children of the Universe. Let that, and that alone, be
the wave that we ride upon! In that very real sense all of life is
spiritual and is to be lived as such. Spiritual awareness begins in
our relationship with self, with family, then with our neighbors,
and extends to the collective.

· Living very high spiritual standards of morality and love, with
caring and responsibility, now and at all times, is the only way to
bring peace and harmony to our planet Earth. No one ever said
that it would be easy.

· While on Earth each of us is a player in a spiritual drama not
fully knowing who we are, where we are going, what our script is,
and how it will all turn out. The more that we can find out about
the storyline on which this brief script is based, the better we can
fill in our part of the drama. We ought never to be completely
preoccupied with our job, our marriage, parenthood, and even
retirement. It is good to think about the part of the cycle of life
that we bring to the Other Side. Thought is to be given to a
more complete picture of our spiritual evolution and the
ongoing story it tells.

- Have we tried to understand the entire picture and then place this brief time of physical life on Earth in perspective? Only then can it all begin to make sense. We can never fairly judge a play by the first minute. How can we hope to judge earthly life or eternal spiritual reality by a very, very brief lifetime within the overall reality of cosmic time? Spiritual reality is so much greater than we can ever know in our brief time on Earth.
- Life on Earth must be structured in smaller communities within larger communities within still larger communities. That is our future if we are to survive.
- The basis of spiritual growth is the knowledge that our soul is a vehicle of love and is forever and ever. Each Earthly incarnation allows us to mature and come closer to the eternal One and the eternal One's creations. This current journey is too precious to waste on hate, greed, drugs, bigotry, alcohol, narrow thinking, hubris, or even boredom. A wasted incarnation will make the next one even more difficult.

". . . the essential message of all religions is very much the same.
They all advocate love, compassion, and forgiveness.
And even those who do not believe in religions can appreciate
the virtues of basic human values."
—THE DALAI LAMA

- If we lived each moment in a state of loving God and all of God's creations, we would be in a state of total unity that is also a state of endless joy.
- Within each of us is the call to return to our creator, not to be absorbed, but rather to be in loving relationship. This return begins with caring for self and the individual next to us. It is that simple and that awesome.

- The first time that you inwardly knew that you were a Child of God was the most life-changing moment of your existence! The next life-changing moment occurred when you realized that all of us, without exception, are also Children of God! We are all created with the sparks of the eternal One.
- Humans ought not to become slaves to gratification of their physical bodies.
- It is only proper to ask for help from Above after we have taken the first step toward resolution.
- There is the appearance of the beautiful. Your constant task is to pierce that appearance and to locate the reality. The reality is always the spark of the eternal One. It has been so for all time.
- To be blind to the Oneness of the spiritual is to be truly living a life in darkness.
- Religion can be a threat to each of us if it steals us away from humanity and makes us its own. It can be a glorious gift if it teaches us brotherhood and takes us to the gateway to the Divine. The best way for us to approach the eternal One is the path that we select in loving action. There is no one path that is better than all others. We are all in different states of spiritual maturity (consciousness).
- All noble action is threefold. There is the I–Thou relationship of the two parties, and there is always the spirit hovering and encompassing.
- We are always connected to two worlds with differing foundations of thought and logic. On Earth we generally observe analytically and intuitively. On the Other Side action and thought are always based on love. The closer that we come to thinking in love as well as intellect, the closer we come to the spiritual. That thinking might be called "the intelligence of love." We fully connect to the spiritual only by thinking and acting in Love. There is no other way.

- After the creation of the souls it was clear that a physical universe was needed in order for souls to mature spiritually. A physical school was needed for physical experiences. The physical universe and the Other Side are both places for growth when we use them wisely. They are necessities for climbing the ladder of spiritual maturity.

- It seems to me—and this is only conjecture, because none of us can know the thoughts of the eternal One—that the fundamental gift from the eternal One is our free will and the responsibility for our actions. This means to me that the eternal One wants those who, in freedom, choose to be with God in love and truth to be able to do so. We begin this journey by loving the creations of the eternal One.

- Individual free will is at the core of human existence. This gift of free will is balanced by absolute responsibility for our actions. That balance is beautiful in conception and actuality. We are free to act, and we are responsible for our choices and actions. That requires of us a balanced intelligence to fully understand the nature of freedom as *love in action.* Act in love of God and in love for all of God's creations. We will not fully understand how to live our lives until we realize that we are supported by the pillars of free will and responsibility. They must always be in equality and balance. We achieve our freedom by using our free will to think and act in love. Free will without caring and responsibility is chaos!

- Our choice is clear. Grow toward God as the Light, or hide in the shadows of the self-centered ego. That is the fundamental choice for each of us. The noble choice is made daily by loving God's creatures and the world that we all inhabit. We can evaluate our life by realizing that the quality of our relationships is always at the center. We fulfill our task by being loving, caring, and responsible for the each and the all. There are no exceptions. That is our great leap forward on the path to the eternal One.

- Misuse of our God-given talents deprives us and others of God-given blessings. Only a very self-centered choice counsels us to act in such a manner.
- To be knowledgeable of our Wisdom traditions (profound statements over time), wherever found, is a sure way to avoid the narrowness of fundamentalism and the aggressiveness of fanaticism.
- I pray that as more people have an awareness of the cycle of life and as we achieve an understanding that we are all on individual, positive missions here on Earth, it will lead to far more significance paid to our active Earthly and Spiritual growth through the power of love.
- The names and attributes of God in Hebrew, Islam, Christianity, Buddhism, and Hinduism's sacred literature number more than two hundred. These can all be condensed into one: LOVING WITHOUT END.

My dear friend Jeff asked me the following very appropriate two questions. Lorraine provided the answers:

1) Why is there a veil between Earth and the Other Side?

The veil has existed so that there would be a formidable separation between the Earth and This Side. That way we have free choice in all of our decisions on Earth since we would not feel that we are part of the spiritual world. Free will and responsibility are essential for spiritual growth. It had to be this way in order to enable us to go forward toward freedom. Only with free choice are we able to make our own decisions, often for very wrong reasons. As we mature spiritually the wall begins to crumble.

We grow stronger, spiritually, by overcoming weaknesses, which can only be brought to our attention in a physical incarnation without direct knowledge of the spiritual domain. There are now cracks in the veil simply because humans require assurance that they are truly spiritual beings in a physical incarnation. Most humans have not been able to climb the ladder without assistance. As a civilization we have had our heroes, but they have been few and far between. As a civilization we needed help very badly. It is now being provided.

2) Why do we "forget" about the Other Side when we are on Earth?

For the very same reasons why we have had a veil. The physical body never had knowledge of This Side. The soul always does but the physical body rarely wants to listen.

If the physical body always acted in love it would climb the spiritual ladder toward freedom and would listen to its soul. There would be a genuine awakening based on noble living. Pain, in the physical incarnation, is sometimes necessary for spiritual growth. If we are unaware of This Side, our best guides to action on Earth are love and caring. This is why we "forget." It always has to do with our free choice of actions and thoughts. It has always been this way in order that we may climb toward freedom, always acting in love, always free to choose. Freedom and spiritual action are two names for the same event. We "forget" so that we may mature. Freedom, always acting in love, had to be earned in order for it to be our forever attribute. If freedom were given to us it would not be appreciated, and we would be weak without courage to act. We could never attain status as a co-creator with the Oneness.

I have read *The Tibetan Book of the Dead* and *The Egyptian Book of the Dead*. These two, and now *The Western Book of Crossing Over*, present differing views of spiritual reality after the physical dimension is left behind. Assuming all three to be accurate in the initial stages of crossing over, do you think there is a spiritual reality beyond their individual realities?

I now know that there is. The three are then gateways to the One.

The more that we observe life, the more we realize that there are two paths opened before us: The first path, generally the current direction of many people, increases our need for materialism, greed, manipulation of others, and a thirst for power. The second path, the more difficult path but one filled with an inner peace, has us seeking spiritual growth with a harmony of joy. It is the path of the self-realized individual. We have many such models throughout history. It may be called the self-realized one, the enlightened Being, the avatar, cosmic consciousness, the Cosmic Christ principle, the Anointed One, Buddha Consciousness, soul consciousness, the Initiate, and so on. These are but names for the same attainment. Some of the individuals we might cite are Buddha, Krishna, Moses, Jesus, and Mohammad. In peak moments we, as individuals, participate in their consciousness at whatever level is possible to us according to our spiritual intentions and efforts. We can measure our spiritual maturation as honest seekers on our spiritual return to awareness of our Oneness by our expansion of consciousness.

In each of us, male and female alike, deep inside lies our cosmic consciousness (our higher self, spark, or soul) awaiting release through our own labors. This is our chief and necessary task at this time in our own and the Earth's evolution. (The Earth was planned for evolution.)

I have wondered why this profound information provided in these last few pages was not provided for me earlier in the writing of this book. I sought clarification in meditation. It became clear and so obvious. In this time of our civilization what we need, perhaps as never before in our history, is the realization of the female energy—Shechinah, Goddess, Sophia, Venus, Isis, Lakshmi, or Divine Mother—and what she has always

meant to us. Our time needs all of us to fill ourselves with love and compassion for all of the creations of the eternal One, and to act toward all
others with the love and compassion that has been heaped upon us.
Such love and compassion has always been our support and salvation.
It must be our very substance today. It must be. Providing this information at the book's closing made it very easy to remember. It left a
strong message to consider.

The universe was born in love and is sustained in love.
The universe was born in love and is sustained in love.

That which enabled this "transmission" from the Other Side was achieved
after years of meditation and contemplation. If we are to move forward
it will mean a truly expanded consciousness gliding on the wings of love.
Let that also be our voice and our action!

APPENDIX: A CHRONOLOGY

On August 27, 2002, our wedding anniversary, in my meditation, Lorraine and I met by a small waterfall in our thirteen-acre forest in Ithaca, New York. Lorraine was wearing her Native American dress. We hugged and kissed and then hugged and kissed some more. She was very animated. We each said "I love you" many times. When we quieted down, I again asked her if she really wanted to do the new book since much would fall on her shoulders. She eagerly said, "Yes, yes" and then again, "yes, yes."

September 25, 2002: 5:45 a.m. Lorraine provided a fascinating bit of information. It absolutely amazed me. She said that we programmed her early "passing back over" prior to our incarnating on Earth. We did this so that she would be able to provide insights from the Other Side that are usually unavailable to us while in a physical incarnation. *Universal Kabbalah: Dawn of a New Consciousness* and this book are then a major part of our tikkun! We must have seen great importance for these books while still on the Other Side. The importance was all about helping people right here on Earth live noble lives. In these books we stressed that there is a fundamental sanctity to all relationships. Relationships are sacred and are essential to our lives. Love and compassion are at the core of any life and civilization. This must become a major theme in all of life, and it must begin during childhood and continue through the years of formal education. Education can present these concepts in either of the following ways:

All of life is a physical as well as spiritual encounter. We are spiritual beings having a physical experience for our mature growth.
Life, at all levels, must be lived in a sustainable way. This can only be done by living continuous I–Thou relationships with all

people, with all nature, and with all of creation. The essence of life is the quality of our relationships at all levels of our lives.

My thoughts and her information from the Other Side placed all understanding in a new and wonderful light.

It is now clear that we have been given "free will" at all times and in all dimensions, the transitory and the permanent. We could always have changed our minds and gone in other directions if we so wished. This also points out the great amount of work our guides needed to do prior to our incarnation in order for it all to have a possibility of coming together.

April 24, 2003. I stopped at my cousin Nancy Cohen's house in Great Neck, New York. Nancy is a wonderful person who happens to be a fine medium. I was on my way to spend a weekend with my son Joshua and his family. While seated on Nancy's lawn, I asked of her a "reading." That experience included a visit with Lorraine, who always provided some validation so we would be sure that the communication was authentic. This time, Lorraine showed roses and wished Joshua a loving birthday. Joshua's birthday was a month away, but I had brought a birthday cake and a present for him since I didn't know if I would be down from Ithaca on his birthday. Lorraine clearly knew of the cake and present.

She also told Nancy that my brother Larry and I would be taking a "long trip together." Again, right. Larry and I did make a trip to India in the subsequent months. Lorraine also wanted me to "get the Kabbalah book reviewed by a medium." That seemed reasonable since she wanted someone with a consciousness able to fully understand what the book was all about. I asked Nancy if she would do so and she gladly agreed. Lorraine also said that she was helping young soldiers who were passing over from the war in Iraq. That kindness was very typical of her.

Now her thoughts on the new book flowed and she laid out for me what was yet to come. Again, this second book is to awaken and help people find meaning and purpose in their lives, like the first. We hope that in reading the book, there will be the realization that we are all currently in a physical incarnation, and that we each have a unique mission to fulfill—one that cannot be performed by another. Each of us is unique. Our mission may be a simple thing or one of extreme importance, and it is always unique to each individual.

My life has changed significantly since I wrote my Introduction to *The Western Book of Crossing Over: Conversations with the Other Side* in September 2003. You might recall that I have said that prior to Lorraine's crossing over she told friends and relatives that I should remarry, and she reinforced that position after she crossed over.

On my anniversary in 2004 I met Barbara for the first time, and we had a long discussion here in Tucson, Arizona. We began a long series of communications from near and far. She lived with family in California at that time. It became clear to both of us that even though we had never met, for much of our lives we were reading similar material and had engaged in similar career paths over the last forty years. A kind of mystical entanglement was obvious, and love became a dominant factor between us.

We married in May 2005. With a strong bond of love we proceeded to take on a task that we both believed part of our singular mission, and so began a third book, *The Partnership Society*, perhaps a key to a flourishing world community of peace and harmony. This, we believed, would help in a general move toward a deeper comprehension of human potential and the evolution of spiritual consciousness.

—SHELDON STOFF
TUCSON, ARIZONA
FEBRUARY 2007

NOTES

Chapter 1

1. Rabbi Adin Steinsaltz, *The Strife of the Spirit* (Northvale, NJ: Jason Aronson, Inc., 1988), p. 216.

2. Carol Zalesti, *Other World Journeys: Accounts of Near-Death Experience in Medieval and Modern Time* (New York: Oxford University Press, 1987).

3. George Gallup, Jr., *Adventures in Immortality: A Look Beyond the Threshold of Death* (New York: McGraw-Hill Book Company, 1982). Gallup is quoted in Raymond A. Moody, Jr., MD, *The Light Beyond* (New York: Bantam Books, 1988), p. 5.

4. Moody, *The Light Beyond*, pp. 14–15.

5. Raymond A. Moody, Jr., MD, *Life After Life* (New York: Bantam Books, 1975), p. 184.

6. Rabbi Lawrence Kushner, *Honey from the Rock* (Woodstock, VT: Jewish Lights Publishing, 1977, 1990), p. 62.

7. Ibid., p. 75.

8. Joseph Head and S.L. Cranston, *Reincarnation: The Phoenix Fire Mystery* (New York: Julian Press/Crown Publishers, Inc., 1977), pp. 407, 408.

9. Ibid., p. 408.

10. Rabbi David Cooper, *God Is A Verb* (New York: Riverhead Books, 1997), p. 269.

11. Rabbi Michael Berg, *The Way: Using the Wisdom of Kabbalah for Spiritual Transformation and Fulfillment* (New York: John Wiley and Sons, Inc., 2001), p. 86.

12. Dr. Rudolf Frieling, *Christianity and Reincarnation* (Edinburgh: Floris Books, 1977), p. 7.

13. Dr. Quincy Howe, Jr., *Reincarnation for the Christian* (Wheaton, IL: The Theosophical Publishing House, 1974), p. 19.

14. Dr. Helen Wambach, *Life Before Life* (New York: Bantam Books, 1979), p. 28.

15. Rabbi Nissen Mangel, trans., *Siddur Tehillat Hashem* (Brooklyn, NY: Merkos L'Inyonel Chinuc, Inc., 1987), p. 118.

Chapter 2

1. Rabbi DovBer Pinson, *Reincarnation and Judaism: The Journey of the Soul* (Jerusalem: Jason Aronson, Inc., 1999).

2. Joel L. Whitton, MD, PhD, *Life Between Life: Scientific Explorations into the Void*
_____. *Separating One Incarnation from the Next* (New York: Warner Books, 1986), p. 57.

3. Rabbi Adin Steinsaltz, *The Thirteen-Petalled Rose* (New York: Basic Books, Inc., 1980), pp. 101–102, 134.

4. Ibid., p. 134.

5. Martin Buber, *I and Thou* (New York: Charles Scribner's Sons, 1958), pp. 115–116.

6. Rabbi Michael Berg, *The Way: Using the Wisdom of Kabbalah for Spiritual Transformation and Fulfillment* (New York: John Wiley and Sons, Inc., 2001), p. 210.

SUGGESTED READING

Berg, Rabbi Michael. *The Way: Using the Wisdom of Kabbalah for Spiritual Transformation and Fulfillment*. New York: John Wiley and Sons, Inc., 2001.

Bohm, David. *Wholeness and the Implicate Order*. Boston: Routledge & Kegan Paul, 1980.

Braden, Gregg. *The Divine Matrix: Bridging Time, Space, Miracles, and Belief*. Del Mar, CA: Hay House, 2007.

Buber, Martin. *Between Man and Man*. New York: Macmillan Publishing Co., Inc., 1975.

Buber, Martin. *Eclipse of God*. New York: Harper Torchbooks, 1952.

Buber, Martin. *I and Thou*. New York: Charles Scribner's Sons, 1958.

Buber, Martin. *Tales of Hasidim: Early Masters*. New York: Schocken Books, 1947.

Buber, Martin. *Tales of Hasidim: Later Masters*. New York: Schocken Books, 1947.

Buber, Martin. *Ten Rungs: Hasidic Sayings*. New York: Schocken Books, 1947.

Budge, Wallis, translator. *The Egyptian Book of the Dead*. New York: Dover Publications, 1967.

Chamberlain, David, PhD. *The Mind of the Newborn Baby*. Berkeley, CA: North Atlantic Books, 1998.

Cooper, Rabbi David. *God Is A Verb*. New York: Riverhead Books, Inc., 1997.

Dalai Lama. Edited by Nicholas Vreeland. *An Open Heart*. New York: Little, Brown and Company, 2001.

Dalai Lama. Translator, Jeffrey Hopkins. *How to Expand Love*. New York: Atria Books, 2005.

Dosick, Rabbi Wayne. *Dancing with God*. San Francisco: Harper-Collins, 1997.

Evans-Wentz, W.Y., translator. *The Tibetan Book of the Dead*. New York: Oxford University Press, 1960.

Frieling, Dr. Rudolf. *Christianity and Reincarnation.* Edinburgh: Furis Books, 1977.

Gallup, George, Jr. *Adventures in Immortality: A Look Beyond the Threshold of Death.* New York: McGraw-Hill Book Company, 1982.

Gikatilla, Rabbi Joseph. Translator, Avi Weinstein. *Gates of Light.* San Francisco: Harper-Collins, 1994. (Originally published in the thirteenth century.)

Gottlieb, Freema. *The Lamp of God.* Northvale, NJ: Jason Aronson, Inc., 1989.

Grof, Stanislav, MD. *Beyond the Brain.* Albany: State University of New York, 1985.

Head, Joseph, and S. L. Cranston, compilers and editors. *Reincarnation: The Phoenix Fire Mystery.* New York: Julian Press/Crown Publishers, Inc., 1977.

Howe, Dr. Quincy, Jr. *Reincarnation for the Christian.* Wheaton, IL: The Theosophical Publishing House, 1974.

Jyoti, Amar. *Retreat into Eternity.* Tucson: Truth Consciousness, 1981.

Kook, Rabbi Abraham Isaac. Translator, Ben Zion Bokser. *The Lights of Penitence.* New York: Paulist Press, 1978.

Kushner, Rabbi Lawrence. *Honey from the Rock.* Woodstock, VT: Jewish Lights Publishing, 1977, 1990.

Laszlo, Ervin. *The Chaos Point: The World at the Crossroads.* New York: Hampton Roads Publishing Co., 2006.

Lewis, C.S. *A Grief Observed.* New York: Bantam Books, 1979.

MacGregor, Dr. Geddes. *Reincarnation in Christianity.* Wheaton, IL: The Theosophical Publishing House, 1978.

Mangel, Rabbi Nissen. *Siddur Tehillat Hashe.* Brooklyn: Merkos L'Inyonel Chinuc, Inc., 1987.

Moody, Raymond A. *Life After Life.* New York: Bantam Books, 1976.

Moody, Raymond A. *Reflections on Life After Life.* New York: Bantam Books, 1977.

Moody, Raymond A. *The Light Beyond.* New York: Bantam Books, 1988.

Morse, Melvin, MD. *Closer to the Light: Learning from the Near-Death Experiences of Children.* New York: Villard Books, 1990.

Morse, Melvin, MD. *Where God Lives.* New York: Cliff Street Books, 2000.

Newton, Michael, PhD. *Journey of Souls: Case Studies of Life Between Lives.* Woodbury, VT: Llewellyn Publications, 2002.

Osis, Karlis, PhD, and Erlendur Haraldson, PhD. *At the Hour of Death.* New York: Avon Books, 1977.

Pinson, Rabbi DovBer. *Reincarnation and Judaism.* Jerusalem: Jason Aronson, Inc., 1999.

Rawlings, Maurice, MD. *Beyond Death's Door.* New York: Bantam Books, 1978.

Sri Aurobindo. *The Ideal of Human Unity.* New York: The Sri Aurobindo Library, 1950.

Steinsaltz, Rabbi Adin. *The Thirteen-Petalled Rose.* New York: Basic Books, Inc., 1980.

Steinsaltz, Rabbi Adin. *The Strife of Spirit.* Northvale, NJ: Jason Aronson, Inc., 1988.

Teilhard de Chardin, Pierre. Translator, J. M. Cohen. *Human Energy.* New York: Harcourt Brace Jovanovich, 1962.

Teilhard de Chardin, Pierre. Translator, Norman Denny. *The Future of Man.* New York: Harper and Row, 1964.

Wambach, Dr. Helen. *Life Before Life.* New York: Bantam Books, 1979.

Weiss, Brian, MD. *Through Time into Healing.* New York: Simon & Schuster, 1992.

Whitton, Joel L., MD, PhD. *Life Between Life: Scientific Explorations into the Void Separating One Incarnation from the Next.* New York: Warner Books, 1986.

Winkler, Franz. *Man: The Bridge Between Two Worlds.* New York: Harper and Row, 1960.

Zalesti, Carol. *Other World Journeys: Accounts of Near-Death Experience in Medieval and Modern Time.* New York: Oxford University Press, 1987.

INDEX

ABOUT THE AUTHOR

Sheldon Stoff, EdD, received his doctorate from Cornell University. He has spent most of his career as an educator and spokesperson for Humanistic Education. He served as the Education Department Chair at Adelphi University for twelve years, receiving the Outstanding Educator of America Award in 1974. He established the International Center for Studies in Dialogue with inspiration from his mentor Martin Buber, the renowned philosopher. Dr. Stoff and his wife, the artist Lorraine Marshak Stoff, raised two sons and retired to a farm in Ithaca, New York, where they lived until Lorraine's "crossing over" in 2001.

Dr. Stoff still lectures regularly on integrating mind, body, and soul in education, most recently at Adelphi University and the University of California, Irvine.